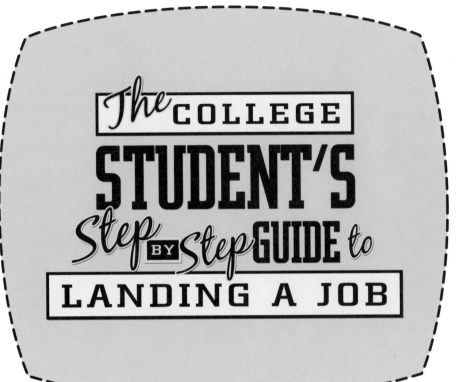

The COLLEGE STUDENT'S Step by Step GUIDE to LANDING A JOB

First printing 2005.

ISBN: 0-9763107-5-9

LCCN: 2004099571

Copyright 2005 Michael T. Krush

All rights reserved

Manufactured in the

United States of America

The paper in this book meets the guidelines for permanence and durability of the
Committee on Production Guidelines for Book Longevity of the Council on Library Resources.

Publisher's Cataloging -in-Publication Data

Krush, Michael T. (Michael Troy), 1971- .

The College Student's Step-By-Step Guide to Landing a Job / by Michael T. Krush.

 p. cm.

Includes an index.

ISBN 0-9763-1075-9 (pbk. : alk. paper)

I. Job hunting.

HF5382.7 .K7874

650.14

ATTENTION CORPORATIONS, UNIVERSITIES, COLLEGES AND PROFESSIONAL ORGANIZATIONS: Quantity discounts are available on bulk purchases of this book for educational, gift purposes, fund-raising activities, or as premiums for increasing magazine subscriptions and renewals. Special books or book excerpts can also be created, at the publisher's discretion, to fit specific needs. For information, please contact the publisher, The Samuel's Intellectual Capital Group, LLC. P. O. Box 217, Greenville, WI 54942.

Dedicated to my
family and friends
who share themselves
and their lives.

Life is too short.
Take a risk and
live it meaningfully.

Thanks mom, dad and Matt.

"Easy to understand and apply. The College Student's Step-By-Step Guide To Landing A Job *understands today's college student's time is precious and it allows you to leverage every minute of your job search for maximum effectiveness."*

— Jim Wessel, Manager.
Big 4 Accounting Firm.

"When I'm interviewing candidates, their level of preparation is the key to landing the job. This book provides the comprehensive preparation all college students need."

— Bryan Christianson, Cerner Corporation.
The leading supplier of healthcare information technology.

"I'd buy The College Student's Step-By-Step Guide To Landing A Job *for my college student on their first day of college."*

— Erik Seidel, Brand Manager.
Kimberly-Clark Corporation, A Fortune 500 Company.

An Invitation

┌─ to The College Student's Step-By-Step
└─ Guide to Landing A Job *Community*

Welcome to...

The College Student's Step-By-Step Guide To Landing A Job. You have invested in yourself, your skills and your career preparation efforts.

You are invited to take part in a unique opportunity. Please accept our official invitation to join our growing community of students from universities, colleges, community colleges and technical/vocational schools.

Go to www.landthatjobonline.com and sign up. Use your The College Student's Step-By-Step Guide To Landing A Job website and make sure to identify the college/university/junior college or technical school you attend.

SIGN UP
www.landthatjobonline.com

When your school reaches 500 members, we'll notify you of a special THANK YOU* seminar in your area.

The seminar will be available at a *significantly discounted rate* to all of the students who purchased the book and registered on-line. In the seminar, you'll learn even more about career preparation and be able to immediately apply your new found knowledge.

*Yes, as usual the small type exists. The COLLEGE STUDENT'S STEP-BY-STEP GUIDE TO LANDING A JOB Thank You Seminars are limited to schools in the U.S. and Canada at this time.

Thanks again for buying
The College Student's Step-By-Step Guide To Landing A Job
and good luck in your career preparation efforts!

Table of Contents

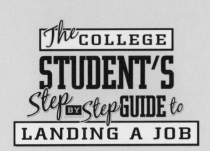

The Right Tool
For The Job

As a college student, I searched for a comprehensive, one-stop career tool kit. I never found it. So I decided to create it.

As you near your final semester, you feel an onrush of emotions–excitement, apprehension and wonder. But most of all, you probably are looking forward to your first job after graduation. After all, over the past three, four, five, six years, you worked diligently to make respectable grades, learn about your industry and even add to your list of accomplishments.

⌐– Have you ever heard the saying, ⌐– "You need the right tool for the job?"

My personal reality check:
When it comes to the job search, many college students find that their learning has just begun. Here are a few of the lessons I learned and wanted to share with you.

⌐– As a college student, I never found the right tool for ⌐– FINDING a job... so I decided to create it.

Lesson 1:
Landing a job requires a significant amount of time.
During your job search, you will balance school, work, extracurricular activities and a social life. Unfortunately, learning about the proper method to effectively land a job is time consuming. You've just added one more task to your priority list. And because preparing for interviews and writing a resumé are often a few months away, it's easy to procrastinate or view it as just another task in your day's busy routine. Needless to say, by procrastinating or not prioritizing your job search ahead of other activities, your potential for successfully landing a job diminishes.

Lesson 2:
The process followed by many college students can be incredibly inefficient and frustrating.
Learning about the job search takes time. On top of your school work, you need to learn to write a resumé and how to act in an interview. Like anyone trying to learn a new skill, it's extremely difficult to absorb the needed information then to immediately and flawlessly execute all of the steps.

On top of learning the skills you need to be successful during the career preparation process, the information you need is sometimes not readily available in one easy-to-understand and comprehensive format. Some students end up sifting through multiple documents, books and seminars to find the key information they need to apply.

The process resembles a jumbled treasure hunt. In this treasure hunt, you first have to find the map and then go searching for the treasure. Needless to say, you might find a few of your friends extremely frustrated and dissatisfied with this process. And as a result some students may default to the quickest and easiest methods. To learn about resumés, they briefly scan a resumé book and attend a quick seminar conducted by their school's placement office. Then, they whip together a resumé. To prospect for jobs, they read a short article which tells them to conduct a job search via a mass mailing. So they spin resumés throughout the country and call five to ten prospective employers a week, with only minimal results.

To learn about interviewing, they briefly talk to the college or university's placement official and learn the basics of an interview. But their schedule provides ample reasons (and sometimes excuses) to not schedule a mock interview. If it won't directly lead to a job offer, your time would be better spent in another activity, right?

After a while, many students become discouraged and feel as though they are constantly searching for direction to no avail. All of their well-intended efforts may not be landing job interviews or the ultimate prize: job offers. *The College Student's Step-By-Step Guide To Landing A Job* helps fix this problem. You will find critical information and indispensible guidance all in a book of approximately 200 pages.

Lesson 3:
The longer it takes to become proficient at your job search, the more opportunities you may lose.
It's very difficult to learn everything you need to know about landing a job in a short period of time. One of the best teachers is experience. And undoubtedly, you will learn how to become more effective in your job search as you experience a number of interviews and countlessly revise your resumé. But unfortunately, time is not on your side in the preparation process. If you choose to polish your interviewing skills through actual interviews with employers, you may not be at your absolute best and may miss great opportunities with the organizations you covet.

Lesson 4:
Landing a job requires the right mindset.
To truly be effective in the career preparation process, you need to change your perspective.

Reflect on this one simple thought: What would happen if you changed your perspective from simply being a job candidate to someone who really understands the craft of job preparation and who takes the time to work on their skills? Instead of simply checking off tasks, such as making a resumé and scheduling interviews, you approach the process as if you are in the midst of crafting something very important (i.e. the perception of prospective employers).

Who better to emulate in this endeavor than the master creators in our world–artists, authors, architects and other craftpersons.
Imagine following the same approach as someone who creates valuable works each and every day, an artisan. Whether it's building a home, painting a picture, writing a song or painstakingly carving a sculpture, the artists, writers and artisans of our world create masterpieces through preparation and specialized tools.

How would your perspective regarding the entire career preparation process change if you adopted a similar mindset? Well, get ready! You are about to try this perspective. As you read *The College Student's Step-By-Step Guide To Landing A Job*, you learn how to try on the hats of the master creators of our world, such as builders, artists and writers. You will leverage their knowledge and borrow their respective approach to learn about yourself and prepare to land a job.

Soon you'll place the same passion, the same understanding, and the same pride in your resumé and interviewing skills as an artist places in her artwork. Your resumé will be transformed from a list of past summer jobs to a living, breathing document that reflects an inherent sense of value to those who view it. A powerful concept? Absolutely.

Lesson 5:
Landing job requires the right tools.
Just imagine if an artist had to literally build her own paintbrush and construct her own canvas before any work could begin. What a ridiculous notion! But wait! In the traditional preparation process, college students often find that they have to search and compile the right information, examples and guides on their own. This effort may take weeks or even months. *The College Student's Step-By-Step Guide To Landing A Job* believes great artisans always have the right tools — tools specifically designed for their craft, tools readily available for each task.

What if you told an artist, it's time to build your own brushes and canvas?

If you truly are going to create a masterpiece, why should you have to search for the guidelines, examples and information you need?

The College Student's Step-By-Step Guide To Landing A Job **provides you with tools designed specifically for college students and their career preparation process.**

That's why you'll find a comprehensive toolkit in approximately 200 pages.

In each chapter, you will learn about methods for successful career preparation ranging from understanding your key skill sets to effectively communicating your value to potential employers.

Plus, you will work with a comprehensive, one-stop tool kit to efficiently integrate your new found learning, *The College Student's Step-By-Step Guide To Landing A Job: Career Toolkit*, which is packed with a number of easy-to-use summaries, worksheets and overviews.

In a short time, you will possess the needed tools to begin to create your own personal works of art, from remarkable resumés to incredible interviewing skills to help you land the job you want.

But remember, your dedication and level of preparation will make the difference in the outcome of your job search. After all, just like any test in school or in life, your grade is up to you.

Congratulations on making the first step forward on your career preparation process.

Good luck.

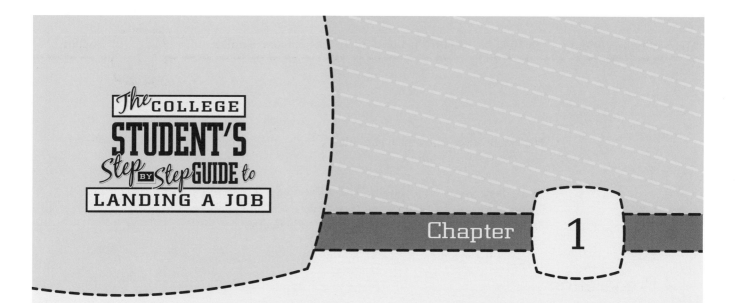

The Architect: Developing A Blueprint For Action

It's time to learn about the plan for your personal career preparation process.

The key to success in any area of life—a big game, a recital or a class project—lies in your level of preparation.

To maximize your preparation, *The College Student's Step-By-Step Guide To Landing A Job* provides you with numerous tools. Each new tool allows you to build on the previous tool and become more efficient and effective.

–– Preparation

The process is similar to building a house. Imagine, if on day one you receive your raw materials. Now imagine, every day you receive a new tool for your toolkit:

> **On day two,** you receive a blueprint to build the house.
> **On day three,** you receive a hammer and nails to connect all of the materials.
> And so on...and so on...
> **On the final day,** you receive a rag to polish your work.

Imagine the monumental progress you make with each new tool. If you had just started with a pile of raw materials and received nothing else–no plan, no hammer, no nails, no tools, the process would be grueling. But by receiving and applying new tools each day, your progress increases exponentially.

This book is developed in the same manner. In each section, you will receive a new tool. Each new tool focuses on a specific element of the career development process. Additionally, you will find a number of templates and samples, which are intended to help you connect the concept with your personal experiences and apply your newfound learning as well as increase your efficiency. By the end of the book, you will possess a toolkit full of skills and knowledge, and more importantly, you will be able to apply it to your upcoming career quest.

Your first step is to change your mindset. In the upcoming chapters, you will follow the process of some of the finest master creators in our world, the artists, crafters and builders. The first master creator whose perspective you will adopt is an architect. Architects take their imagination, their ingenuity and their creativity and develop plans, known as blueprints. Blueprints guide builders and contractors through the process of creating something spectacular.

In your case, *The College Student's Step-By-Step Guide To Landing A Job* has taken the liberty to help get you started. *The College Student's Step-By-Step Guide To Landing A Job* introduces you to the first plan, a masterful plan centered around your personal career preparation process. The plan shows the upcoming career preparation process you will be taking. In fact, if you were to review a blueprint of the entire process, it would resemble the overview on the following page.

Section I
The College Student's Step-By-Step Guide To Landing A Job: Career Toolkit

In the first section of this book, you will be introduced to *The College Student's Step-By-Step Guide To Landing A Job:* Career Toolkit, a tool designed to efficiently guide you through the entire career preparation process.

The College Student's Step-By-Step Guide To Landing A Job: Career Toolkit contains a variety of templates, schedules and guides in one centralized location (the back of the book). As you page through *The College Student's Step-By-Step Guide To Landing A Job:* Career Toolkit, you will notice worksheets, templates and guides that will allow you to immediately apply your learning.

The first three steps in *The College Student's Step-By-Step Guide To Landing A Job:* Career Toolkit center on helping you understand more about you.

Gathering the Raw Materials of Your Life: This is a brainstorming exercise designed to help you understand your life experiences and accomplishments.

Adding Perspective About You: In this section, you'll find tools to help you develop a structure around your experiences, accomplishments and skills.

The DART Principle: In this section, you will learn and use a tool that can help you concisely communicate the value of your skills and experiences.

Section II
Understanding Your Trade and Your Buyer
This section provides you with the tools you need to effectively understand the position and industry you covet. You will learn various ways to research potential career opportunities, the industries in which they operate and the key skills employers seek.

Section III
Crafting Written Communication
In Section III, you will begin to apply your new found knowledge and begin to craft glowing written communication, including resumés, cover letters and thank you notes.

Section IV
Polishing Your Verbal Communication
In the final section, you will begin to expand your career preparation skills. You will learn about the various types of employer interviews, how to prepare for the interviews, the value of mock interviews and successful scheduling strategies.

Apprenticeships

Before many artists or builders master a craft, they usually work with an experienced mentor. During the mentoring process, the apprentice receives the proper training and learns the methods and intricacies related to the craft. With the mentor's assistance and careful guidance, the apprentice minimizes the number of mistakes and the time required to learn the craft.

Actively use this book and its guides, examples and templates.

Write directly in the book!

The College Student's Step-By-Step Guide To Landing A Job also uses Apprenticeships throughout each section. After all, apprenticeships are an incredibly powerful way to become more efficient in the craft. By using this approach, *The College Student's Step-By-Step Guide To Landing A Job* exposes you to a wide range of examples and approaches to help you complete each exercise. The Apprenticeships also provide guidance and direction to increase your efficiency.

When you see the logo,

-- APPRENTICESHIP --

you will know it's time for additional mentoring.

Maximizing The Value of
The College Student's Step-By-Step Guide To Landing A Job

Actively Use This Book

This book's objective is to help you become more proficient and efficient in the career preparation process. To make this book a great investment, you must challenge yourself to read the material actively and follow the five ground rules below.

Suspend judgement of yourself.
In the introduction, you were challenged to change your perspective. When you are developing your resumé and interviewing skills, take the approach of an artist or builder. Approach the project as if you are crafting a work of art, a sculpture, or a custom home–a piece of work that will reflect you and be displayed to a broader audience. A piece of work of which you will truly be proud.

Push yourself beyond your comfort zone.
You also need to push yourself beyond your traditional limits. Many of us have been blessed with our own quality control, a personal filter. Personal filters limit our thoughts. We allow our own inhibitions to curtail our personal creativity and our ability to outwardly express ourselves. You need to rid yourself of this personal filter because many of the initial activities ask you to brainstorm. The value to brainstorming is quantity–the sheer volume of ideas. To effectively brainstorm, please capture every idea which enters your mind. Do not throw a bucket of water on a single creative spark. Do not judge yourself. Get excited and creative about this process. Your progress will amaze you. You will find that the more ideas you generate, the more valuable you will become on paper and in person.

Enjoy becoming the expert on yourself.
Approach each step with a positive attitude. As you complete each exercise, you'll create a collection of history and information about yourself. This increased understanding will become an asset during the career preparation process.

Follow the steps, learn from the examples, and use the tools.
As you probably noticed, *The College Student's Step-By-Step Guide To Landing A Job* continually asks you to actively use this book, make the necessary arrangements and complete the assessments, templates, guides and schedules. These tools were designed specifically for you. Feel free to write in *The College Student's Step-By-Step Guide To Landing A Job: Career Toolkit*. This will allow you to maintain all of your essential career preparation in one location.

Make the most of your investment.
You invested a decent amount of money in this book (at least a night or two of pizza), so please make the most of your investment. Harness the tools and the results will amaze you.

Good Luck!

Chapter Summary

The Architect: Developing A Blueprint For Action

This book understands you have many priorities. That's why it's designed to maximize your efficiency.

The College Student's Step-By-Step Guide To Landing A Job process is divided into four key sections.

Section 1: You are introduced to *The College Student's Step-By-Step Guide To Landing A Job:* Career Toolkit. *The College Student's Step-By-Step Guide To Landing A Job:* Career Toolkit provides you with an opportunity to learn about yourself by providing a centralized location for you to collect your skills, experiences and accolades.

Section 2: In this section, you will learn to efficiently conduct research on the position and industry you covet.

Section 3: You will learn to apply your new found knowledge to expertly craft strong written communication.

Section 4: You will apply this knowledge to hone your verbal communication skills.

Throughout *The College Student's Step-By-Step Guide To Landing A Job*, you will be guided with apprenticeships which mentor you through the process. Each apprenticeship provides you with directions to maximize your efficiency.

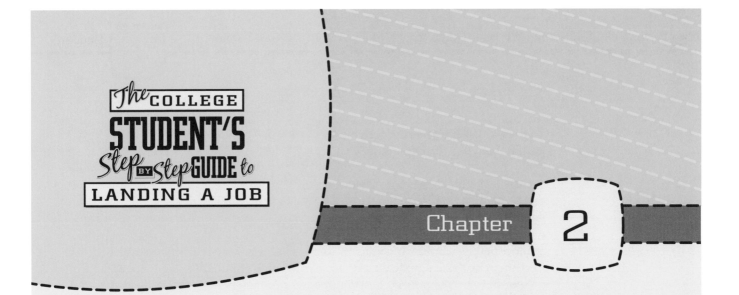

Collect the Raw Materials of Your Life

The first step in efficient career preparation is to compile your skills and experiences.

Your First Tool: Gathering Raw Materials...your life experiences

An artist who builds a home, throws a
piece of pottery, crafts a cabinet, or composes a song starts with raw materials. Raw materials serve as the building blocks, the very essence of any creation. The more diverse the composition of raw materials, the more interesting and valuable the final product becomes. And who better to know about raw materials than a carpenter. The carpenter devotes a significant amount of time ensuring that the right materials are present to begin the project. Learning midway through a project that the right electrical wire, unique granite for countertops or special fixtures are missing is costly. The project could be delayed and additional costs incurred. Thus, the best carpenters understand the value of proactively collecting all of the required raw materials at the beginning rather than midway through the project.

Gather and consolidate your life experiences and skills.
They will become the valuable building blocks
that employers seek.

Throughout your life, you gain skills and experiences. Think about them as building blocks, RAW MATERIALS OF YOUR LIFE.

Your goal lies in compiling and understanding all of your skills and experiences in one central place and then chiseling them into value.

Now, let's apply this approach to you. During the career preparation process, you need to collect all of your raw materials. In this case, your skills and abilities serve as the building blocks for your impending career. While your building blocks may not be as tangible as a load of cement or bricks, they are vastly more valuable to your ultimate buyer, an employer.

However, very few students formally review and compile their skills, experiences and abilities. Without a formalized process or blueprint, they often forget their applicable skills and experiences. Then, during an interview they miss an opportunity to communicate their valuable skills to a prospective employer. Whether you are a carpenter building homes or a carpenter of your career preparation, a slight oversight incurs costs. For the carpenter, the project is delayed. For the college student, an oversight means a missed job opportunity and potentially thousands of dollars in income.

The goal of this chapter is to ensure that you avoid any of these oversights. In this chapter, you will collect and centralize your skills, experiences and abilities.

This chapter is known as the RAW MATERIALS OF YOUR LIFE portion of *The College Student's Step-By-Step Guide To Landing A Job*: Career Toolkit. Take a moment to turn to the last section of the book, *The College Student's Step-By-Step Guide To Landing A Job*: Career Toolkit. In the first section, you will find a table.

On the far left column, you will see a section named, the RAW MATERIALS OF YOUR LIFE. This section is comprised of a series of questions that are intended to spur your memory of an event or action. After you read the question, you will write in column two whatever experience(s) pop into your mind.

Step 1:

You will see a table divided into four columns. You will read the first column, the RAW MATERIALS OF YOUR LIFE. The RAW MATERIALS OF YOUR LIFE questions are intended to spur your memory of an event or action. The goal is to complete as many questions as possible. The order of completion is irrelevant. Begin at the top of the list, the middle of the list or the bottom of the list. Left-brained, right-brained, slob, anal retentive...this exercise welcomes all.

Step 2:

After you read a question, write the related event(s) and experience(s) that come to mind in the section next to the question. Capture any idea and/or event that occurs to you. Don't worry if your example is not perfectly related. The objective of this exercise is to stimulate thought through brainstorming.

Step 3:

Your notes should concisely capture the essence of the experience. Target 7-15 words per event. After you write your answer, ask yourself if you would understand the information if you read it tomorrow. If you would not understand the information, write a few additional words to better describe the event.

Step 4:

Capture as many ideas as possible. In this exercise, you create value with the pure quantity of ideas and experiences you cite. It's possible you may write several examples in response to some questions, while in other sections you may not have any examples.

> The key to the RAW MATERIALS OF YOUR LIFE section is pure quantity of ideas and diversity of thought. Write whatever experience or story comes into your mind as you review the questions.

Step 5:

Don't judge yourself or filter any ideas. In many instances, you may say, "I only had a 2.8 GPA, this isn't important enough to write it down." Baloney. Write down 2.8 GPA and move on to the next idea.

Step 6:

Take the next 15 to 45 minutes to write out your answers to the following questions. When you are finished, STOP. Break away from the exercise for at least one hour.

After your break, begin reviewing the exercise again. Devote 15 to 45 minutes to this review. Capture any additional notes or examples. The additional review may spur your creativity. Then, complete any unfinished sections.

APPRENTICESHIP

Great Master Creators usually serve apprenticeships before they practice their craft on their own. The mentor provides the apprentice with guidance, suggests potential approaches and passes along helpful hints to increase the apprentice's efficiency.

You will find several apprenticeships throughout the upcoming chapters. The examples provide various approaches and are intended to provide guidance rather than specific direction.

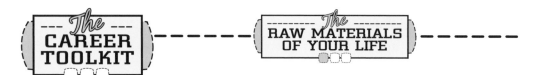

THE CAREER TOOLKIT — **THE RAW MATERIALS OF YOUR LIFE**

Example 1

In what, if any, Honor Societies have you been a member?

High School: National Honor Society. Johnson High School Inducted in 1999. **1**

College: Omnicron Delta Epsilon, Jackson College. Inducted 2001. Top 8% of junior class. **2**

On a performance evaluation, did you ever receive the highest rating possible, such as an "exceeds expectations"?

College internship with Majors Power, Inc. Received exceeded expectations. Received job offer from company after internship. Summer 2002. **3**

Explanation

The examples provide one approach to the exercise.

1. Use specific words and be concise.
In this example, the response is direct. The student names the honor society, the high school attended and the date of induction.

2. Describe the honor/experience.
In less than 15 words, the student highlights the honor, the college attended, the date of the award and the requirements for induction.

3. Discuss performance.
The example provides the date of the internship, the employer and an interesting fact. The student received an exceeded expectations on her performance review and the company offered her a position upon graduation.

Please note, this tool is not a test. Think quantity: The student provided two examples for the first question. You may write numerous examples for one question while you may not be able to provide any example for other questions. Remember, this is a brainstorming activity. Do not attempt to answer the questions like a test. No right answers exist. Even if your skills and experiences do not exactly answer the questions, you still receive and A for its completion.

-- APPRENTICESHIP --

APPRENTICESHIP

A few more examples follow for your reference as you complete the RAW MATERIALS OF YOUR LIFE section.

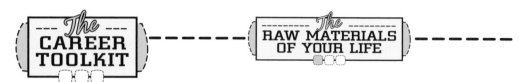

Please list any leadership activities within a civic, charity, or volunteer organization in which you have participated.	*Foothills Softball Association Treasurer. 2003. In charge of all budgets for Junior baseball.* *Volunteer coordinator. Alpha Zi Gamma Walk for Life. 2003. Raised $1000 dollars for American Lung Society.*
List any of the following creative activities in which you participate or have participated. 1) Drawing 2) Graphic arts 3) Painting 4) Sculpture 5) Photography 6) Other endeavors	*High School: (Nola High School)* *1) Painting class. Received A. 1999* *2) Photography class. 2000. A-.* *College: (Univ. of Elka)* *1) Desktop publishing class. A. 2001* *2) Designed a brochure for student activities office. 2002.*

Chapter Summary

Collect The Raw Materials Of Your Life

All great artists start with raw materials:
The master creators in our world start with raw materials, the very building blocks of a soon-to-be masterpiece.

In this exercise, you will take the perspective of a carpenter:
Great carpenters understand the value of proactively assembling all of their raw materials. An oversight of a needed material can cost time and money.

The RAW MATERIALS OF YOUR LIFE are your skills, experiences and abilities:
As the artist of your own career, your skills, experiences and abilities serve as the basic building blocks of your career. Hence, the first step is to collect all of your skills, experiences, accolades and abilities in a central place, the Raw Materials of Your Life section in *The College Student's Step-By-Step Guide To Landing A Job: Career Toolkit.*

The RAW MATERIALS OF YOUR LIFE section is a brainstorming section:
Read each question and write whatever experience(s) immediately pop into your mind. For some questions you may write multiple examples, while other questions may only stimulate a few examples.

Quantity is key:
Avoid judging yourself during this exercise. Remember, the sheer quantity and diversity of ideas is the key to the exercise.

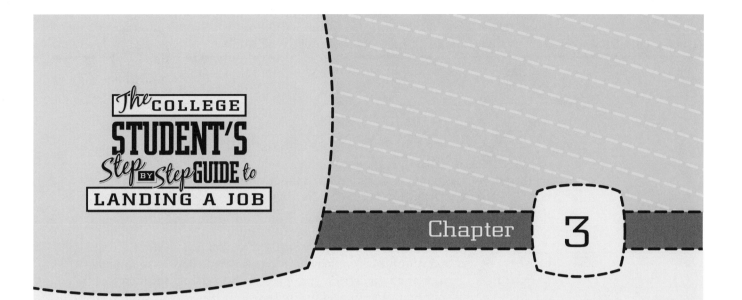

Adding Perspective: Learning About Yourself

In this chapter, you will learn to add essential details to your skills and experiences.

A Quick Review of Your Accomplishments & Helpful Hints.

In the previous section, you began to learn about yourself by completing the RAW MATERIALS OF YOUR LIFE portion of *The College Student's Step-By-Step Guide To Landing A Job: Career Toolkit.*

After a few hours or maybe even days, you reviewed the questions and your ideas. You may have even written a few more examples. Now, as you reflect on your progress, you should be impressed by your brainstorming efforts. In fact, your hard work thus far will help you successfully complete the future exercises and your career preparation as a whole.

–– Adding form to your experiences and skills

Approach the project like an ARTIST.

In the next step of *The College Student's Step-By-Step Guide To Landing A Job*, you will try on the proverbial hat of an artist. When an artist receives her materials, inks, watercolors, canvas and brushes, she may begin by sketching on a pad or a canvas, before she begins to paint. Perhaps, she outlines the horizon, sketches the background of the scene or adds dimension to the objects. She is developing a context, a rough template which aids her in understanding how each of her raw materials comprises the whole structure. As she does this, the artist begins to discover how the entire work will eventually look.

Your approach will be similar to an artist. You will begin to sketch the details of your career masterpiece. You will add perspective to your experiences, skills and accolades. In *The College Student's Step-By-Step Guide To Landing A Job* jargon, it's called, ADDING PERSPECTIVE ABOUT YOU.

How to Add Form.

In this section, ADDING PERSPECTIVE, you will structure your experiences, skills and abilities in a meaningful way. You will add stronger details and more precise descriptions to each of the examples in the RAW MATERIALS OF YOUR LIFE section.

You will be see a range of questions to help you add these details. The questions are your specialized tools for this exercise. For instance, some questions will ask you to describe the dates, locations and results for each of your life experiences.

By using these questions, you may find yourself adding a number of details to your role in a volunteer activity; providing a stronger description of how much money you raised during an art exhibition; and describing why you received an academic award.

Your Tools For This Activity:

To increase your efficiency in completing this exercise, a checklist of questions follows. The questions are intended to help you further describe each example in the RAW MATERIALS OF YOUR LIFE section. The checklist includes one key question and then a few potential methods to answer the question.

How To Complete This Activity:

1) Turn to *The College Student's Step-By-Step Guide To Landing A Job:* Career Toolkit.

2) Read over your first answer in the RAW MATERIALS OF YOUR LIFE section.

3) Your goal is to provide a stronger description of each example in the ADDING PERSPECTIVE ABOUT YOU column.

4) You will accomplish this by reviewing the checklist of questions and attempting to answer as many of the questions for each example as possible. As you will see, examples of potential answers are provided after each question.

Oh yeah...one other suggestion...or maybe two suggestions.
This activity is similar to the RAW MATERIALS OF YOUR LIFE section. Quantity counts and free associations are welcome. Do not judge your thoughts. Write whatever comes into your mind.

The entire activity should take no more than 60 – 90 minutes.

ADDING PERSPECTIVE ABOUT YOU Checklist

Who was involved?
Example: I was a member of a class, a team, an organization, a business, an internship, a summer job.

What was my role?
Example: My title was _____ .
Example: My job description was _____ .
Example: I was responsible for _____ .

When did it occur?
Example: It occurred during/on _____ .

Why did I do it?
Example: I was motivated by _____ to do this.
Example: This _____ was part of my job responsibilities.
Example: I took it upon myself to do this task because _____ .
Example: This was an activity I did on my own initiative because _____ .
Example: Was I one of a few to do this activity? _____
Example: This was important because _____ .

What was the goal?
Example: The ____ problem/opportunity existed and needed to be overcome/realized.
Example: I was told to do this.

How did it happen?
Example: The background of this activity is _____ .
The activity occurred as part of a class, a job, an internship, an extracurricular activity, a team or event.
Example: The event occurred (when?) _____ .

What was the result?
Example: The team accomplished (what?) goal.
Example: This was the first time a person or team accomplished (what?).
Example: I/the team received a grade, a commendation, kudos from someone.
Example: I learned (what?) from this experience.
Example: The activity continues to occur.
Example: Someone (who/what?) continues to use our work.
Example: How would I state I made a difference?
Example: Did I increase or decrease anything?
Example: Was I one of a few to receive this honor?
Example: Did this activity make an impact on anyone or anything?
Example: Did any quantifiable results occur?
Example: Did this allow me to enter into or take part in something else?

APPRENTICESHIP

Review the following examples.

As you'll note, the RAW MATERIALS OF YOUR LIFE sections are completed. The next step is to complete the ADDING PERSPECTIVE ABOUT YOU section. The examples provide various approaches to answer the questions and an explanation. The intent is to provide you with a flavor for one possible approach.

List any leadership activities within a civic, charity, or volunteer organization in which you have participated	*Foothills Softball Association Treasurer. 2003. In charge of all budgets for Junior baseball. Volunteer coordinator. Alpha Zi Gamma Walk for Life. 2003. Raised $1000 dollars for American Lung Association.*
List all of the school-related leadership activities in which you held a position. (This may include your high school class, student government, student organizations, teams within classes, etc.)	*High school: (Nola High School)* *1) Student government. Junior year.* *2) Senior class president. 1999.* *College: (Univ. of Elka)* *1) Fraternity president. 2001.* *2) Public Relations Society Secretary. 2002.* *3) Account executive in advertising practicum class. John's Ford was client.*
List any of the following creative activities in which you participate or have participated. 1) Drawing 2) Graphic arts 3) Painting 4) Sculpture 5) Photography 6) Other endeavors	*High School: (Nola High School)* *1) Painting class. Received A. 1999.* *2) Photography class. 2000. A-.* *College: (Univ. of Elka)* *1) Desktop publishing class. A. 2001* *2) Designed a brochure for student activities office. 2002.*

APPRENTICESHIP

----ADDING----
PERSPECTIVE

EXPLANATION

Foothills Softball Association, Batter, New Hampshire. **1**
Served as treasurer: 1 year (2003). **2**
Budget Control; maintained spending, fund-raising. **3**
Budget: approximately $20,000.
Key accomplishment: initiated new fund-raiser; **3**
$5,000 increase in funds.
Allowed association to purchase new uniforms. **4**

In this example, the following questions are answered.

1) What organization and where?
2) My Role & When?
3) What I did?
4) What was the impact?

Alpha Zi Gamma Sorority volunteer Coordinator;
Johnson, Idaho. **1**
Chaired sorority's major volunteer event.
Served as coordinator: 2003. **2**
Arranged all logistics; public relations, coordination with
American Lung Association. **3**
200 participants raised $1000 for American Lung Association.
4

In this example, the following questions are answered.

1) What organization and where?
2) What I did and when?
3) How many involved?
4) How many were impacted and the results of my efforts?

Nola High School, Nola, New Hampshire. **1**
Student Government - 2000 (junior year).
2
Represented 400 students.
Junior Class Representative. **3**
Served as representative to PTA; weekly meetings, finance
committee. **4**
Senior Class President - 2001 (senior year). **1**
Represented 200 seniors. **2**
Led all meetings; parliamentary procedure. **4**
Named outstanding senior leader. **5**

In this example, the following questions are answered.

1) What organization and where?
2) Number of people impacted?
3) What was my role?
4) What did I do?
5) How was I recognized?

Chapter Summary

Learning About Yourself

The next step in *The College Student's Step-By-Step Guide To Landing A Job* Career Process is to assume the perspective of an artist.
Once you have collected your experiences and skills in the RAW MATERIALS OF YOUR LIFE section, it's time to provide some form to them.

In the ADDING PERSPECTIVE section, you will begin to add shape to your skills and experience.
To do this, you add context and details to each example.

A set of specialized tools has been developed for this activity.
The key tools at your disposal are a checklist of strong, critical questions to help you develop a broader perspective concerning your skills. Additionally, examples of responses for each question are provided. The examples are intended to provide you with direction.

Complete the ADDING PERSPECTIVE Exercise.
Read over the examples in the Raw Materials of Your Life section, then attempt to answer each of the following questions for each of your previous responses:

Who was involved?

What was my role?

When did it occur?

Why did I do it?

What was the goal?

How did it happen?

What was the result?

The entire activity should take no more than 60 – 90 minutes.

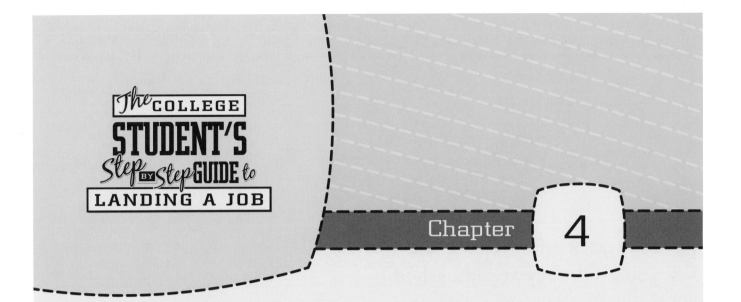

Chapter 4

Perspective & Reflection

You are making strong progress.
Now take a moment to review
your work.

Reflect On Your Work.

Great builders and artists take a moment to objectively reflect on their work. During this time, an artist may choose to review her work and the amount of progress she has accomplished.

Step back and evaluate the work you've already accomplished.

The review allows the artist to look for areas that hold opportunity for improvement. A carpenter may note the framing of a certain room is off kilter. By reviewing progress in the beginning stages, the problem may be easily addressed.

Take a moment to review your work. Look for additional experiences and skills to add or existing examples that can be expanded.

Consider following a similar process in your career preparation. Please take 10 to 30 minutes and review your work in *The College Student's Step-By-Step Guide To Landing A Job:* Career Toolkit.

Give yourself credit for the significant amount of work you've accomplished thus far. As you review each section, you will note you have captured your entire life story in bite-sized pieces, including when you played the cello in fourth grade, when you ran track in high school, when you won the local American Legion scholarship and when you served in the Big Sister/Big Brother program.

Perhaps the RAW MATERIALS OF YOUR LIFE section will stimulate a memory of another life experience that you initially forgot to write in your book.

Also, take one more opportunity to provide more context about each of your life experiences in the ADDING PERSPECTIVE ABOUT YOU section. Please remember, an hour wisely spent by reviewing your work now will save you numerous hours later in the process.

After Your Review.

You undoubtedly should feel as though you are making significant progress. In fact, as you review the two completed sections, you probably will notice you are beginning to possess a stronger understanding of YOU than when you began.

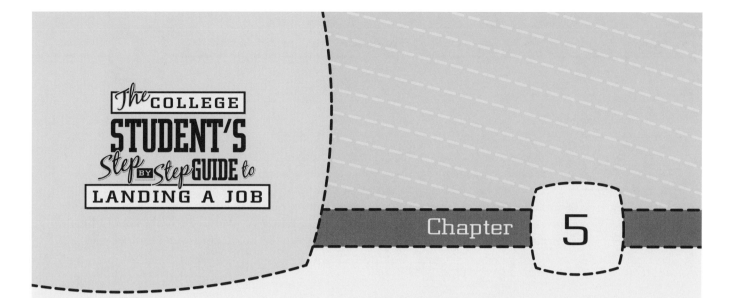

Chapter 5

Creating Great Narrative Using The DART Principle

Use a new tool, the DART Principle, to efficiently describe and compellingly demonstrate your value to employers.

Over the past few chapters, you've assumed the roles of some of the greatest creators in our world, architects, carpenters and artists. And with this perspective, you've made remarkable progress in your career preparation process. You've learned about the value of collecting raw materials and thus you've compiled your skills, accolades and experiences in a central location. You've learned the discipline of an artist, who adds form to her work by sketching out a painting or planning a sculpture. And with this perspective, you've begun to add a greater level of detail around each of your examples.

┌─ Think about the great writers in our world. ──────────

└─ What do they have in common? ──────────────

└─ An ability to create compelling narratives. ──────────

The next step lies in preparing these examples for their final presentation. As the creator of your career, you want these experiences and your value to captivate others–specifically prospective employers. So it makes sense to assume the role of someone who creates enthusiasm in his work, someone skilled at captivating others' interest in learning and in reading.

Who better to emulate in this endeavor than a great writer of literature. After all, think of John Steinbeck, Thoreau, or even contemporaries like John Grisham or Po Bronson. What makes them great? For some, their greatness lies in their ability to invite you inside a story and become part of it. For others, their skills center around finding a way into your heart or your mind. Whatever the method, each great writer creates a compelling narrative that you perceive as valuable.

Your goal as the master creator of your career is to develop compelling narratives about you and your skills, narratives that describe and demonstrate your value and captivate prospective employers. These narratives aren't just statements that appear on ordinary resumés. They describe you and your experiences. The narratives create interest in you and use actual instances to demonstrate your value.

The DART principle teaches you how to craft a compelling narrative about you.

To create compelling narratives, *The College Student's Step-By-Step Guide To Landing A Job* developed a special tool for you: the DART Principle. The DART Principle guides you in developing stories about your skills, your experiences and your honors. The DART Principle's beauty lies in its efficiency. The DART Principle is an easy method to learn and is flexible. You'll be able to apply your learning on resumés, cover letters and during an interview.

As you use the DART Principle, you'll notice that you structure your life experiences in the form of a mini-story. You set the scene (a description), describe your action, tell about the result from your action and close with a synopsis or key take-away.

The Keys to the DART Principle

So let's begin learning how to create great narratives. Let's breakdown the key elements of the DART Principle.

The DART Principle's four major steps follow.

 means Describe:

In the D section, you will write a brief background of the activity. After all, great narratives always begin with an introduction. The introduction sets the scene, introduces the characters and describes the situation.

As a writer of career narratives, you can use the following questions to structure your D.
"When did this occur?"
"Who was involved?"
"What happened?"
"What was the challenge, problem or task?"

You could start your example by DESCRIBING the context or history of a situation and discussing the goal, the opportunity, or the challenge. For instance, you may write, *"For the past two years, I served as the president of the Success University's Art Society. When I started, society membership was 25 and the organization was losing members."*

As you'll note, you are writing about specific prior experiences. Thus, the language will always be in the past tense.

 means Actions.

As you begin to write the A section of each of your career narratives, you'll introduce the reader to your thought process and your action steps.

An effective example will always answer the question, "Due to the situation, what did I do?"

For instance, *"I immediately saw increasing membership as the top priority. By increasing membership we could petition for more funding and offer more activities to our members. I developed a recruiting team, conducted research on what students desired from the club, developed a recruiting plan including faculty and students and implemented nine recruiting activities during the first semester."*

As you'll note, in the action section "I" is the only pronoun used. Employers are trying to understand your specific skills and contributions. Thus, your statements should describe what you personally contributed.

R conveys the Result.

In this section you will convey the outcome as a direct result of your action. An effective example will answer the question, "What happened due to my actions?" or "This is the impact of my actions." In this section, you may also include short term and/or long term results.

In our example, you may write, *"Due to the recruiting activities, membership skyrocketed 100 percent to 50 members. One year later, membership is 100 members. The club has also been recognized as the top club by the Fine Arts Department and I was elected president for a second term."*

Please note the specific results the candidate wrote. Describe any honors received, quantify any increases or relay any commendations from others when possible.

T means the Take-Away.

The take-away is the key element in the DART principle. This element provides a conclusion to your narrative. Think of the T section as the main point. The T section should answer the question, "What makes this example valuable?"

For instance, *"I believe this experience really reaffirmed to me that the keys to leadership are to prioritize, to take initiative and to motivate others to follow the plan. Because, after all, leadership is spoken best by its results and the club's results showed this."*

The T possesses immense value on a resumé and in an interview. If the interviewer is relatively inexperienced, the T helps the interviewer by concisely summarizing the main point.

It's your turn.

Now, it's your turn to practice writing compelling narratives using the DART Principle.

1) Turn to *The College Student's Step-By-Step Guide To Landing A Job:* Career Toolkit.

2) You will now work in the fourth column, titled Creating Great Narratives, The DART Principle.

3) For each of your examples, you will write a narrative using the DART Principle. After each narrative, ask yourself, "Have I used each of the four principles?"

4) While this exercise may be time consuming, it is incredibly valuable. You will be able to apply the DART Principle throughout your resume, your cover letter and during interviews.

5) To give it the time and attention it deserves, this exercise will take approximately two to four hours at a minimum.

Remember, the DART Principle is essential. By investing the time in structuring the statements, you will become more efficient in developing all of the other components in the career preparation process.

Keys to the DART Principle

The key to conveying your value to a prospective employer lies in the structure and content of your statement. A few key tips for structuring your value statements follow.

Always use *I*.
Focus on your contribution to a team, your action to a situation and the results you delivered. Employers are trying to assess your ability and skill set. Therefore, it's imperative to use "I" in your value statements. While you may work in teams, make sure you describe your contribution.

Use past tense verbs.
Your value statements provide an experience or event that demonstrates a skill or behavior. One of the pitfalls for candidates occurs when they use the present tense. This tips interviewers that you don't possess the skill set or haven't had an opportunity to use it. Show your interviewer you possess the needed skill and have previously demonstrated it by using past tense verbs.

> **Your DART Principle Narratives**
>
> Invest the time in developing your DART Principle narratives. As you continue your career preparation process, they will become extremely valuable.

Focus on being concise.
Provide a strong, concise value statement as succinctly as possible. Minimize the use of non-value-added words. After you complete each DART statement, ask yourself the following question, "Could a complete stranger read and understand this information in 90 seconds or less?" Respect that the interviewer's time is precious. Constantly refine your answers. Babble will quickly eliminate you from consideration.

Explain specifically what you did.
Be specific. Outline the key action steps you took. Your goal is to describe how you act, how you analyze, how you process and how you think when faced with various situations.

Make your results crystal clear.
Show concise, specific, meaningful results in the R section of the DART principle. When possible, quantify your results. Describe honors, reaffirmations, accolades and awards.

Focus on the key information. Use specific details.
Capture the strongest details in each portion of the DART. If you can quantify the number of people involved, a budget, your results, an award, the number of people who won an award, the percentile of your ACT or class rank, please do so. It builds credibility. Try to relay as much specific information as you can in each section.

Be creative when you qualify.
In some examples, you will not be able to quantify your results. Use your creativity to help people understand the situation, the background, and your actions. For instance, you may not be able to quantify the results of your participation in a particular volunteer activity. However, can you reasonably state you received a recommendation or acknowledgment from the president of the organization? Perhaps you initiated a new activity for the organization, and the new activity continued for the next three years?

In order to help you understand how to use the DART Principle, an apprenticeship follows. The apprenticeship displays an abbreviated *The College Student's Step-By-Step Guide To Landing A Job:* Career Toolkit with examples showing potential uses of the DART Principle. The examples provide various approaches to answer the questions. The intent is to provide you with guidance rather than specific direction.

-- APPRENTICESHIP --

List any leadership activities within a civic, charity or volunteer organization in which you have participated

Foothills Softball Association Treasurer. 2003. In charge of all budgets for Junior baseball.

Volunteer coordinator. Alpha Zi Gamma Walk for Life. 2003. Raised $1000 dollars for American Lung Society.

List all school related activities in which you held a leadership position.

(This may include your high school class, student government, student organizations, clubs, teams within classes, etc.)

High school (Nola High School)
1) Student government. Junior year
2) Senior class president in 1999.

College: (Univ. of Elka)
1) Fraternity president. 2001
2) Public Relations Society Secretary. 2002.
3) Account executive in Advertising practicum class. John's Ford was client.

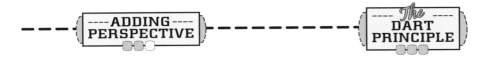

ADDING PERSPECTIVE

Foothills Softball Association, Batter, New Hampshire.
Served as treasurer: 1 year (2003).
Budget Control; maintained spending, fund-raising. Budget: approximately $20,000.
Key accomplishment: initiated new fund-raiser; $5,000 increase in funds.
Allowed association to purchase new uniforms.

The DART PRINCIPLE

Example of my initiative and leadership
Description: *For past three years, Foothills Softball Association could not afford new uniforms for children 8-10. Annual fundraising efforts had been stalled.*
Action: *As newly installed treasurer, had two goals. Ensure spending is controlled and initiate fundraising efforts. Enlisted 12 volunteers, 4 local businesses and all participants. Ensured collaboration of entire committee. Initiated new fundraising effort.*
Results: *Fund-raiser netted $5,000 in funds and allowed uniform purchases. Largest fund-raiser in history of association. Received letter of commendation from association president.*
Takeaway: *I believe a strong key to leadership is initiative as well as collaboration. This example displays my type of leadership.*

Nola High School, Nola, New Hampshire.
Student Government - 1998 (junior year),
Represented 400 students.
Junior Class Representative.
Served as representative to PTA; weekly meetings, finance committee.
Named outstanding junior leader.
Senior Class President - 1999 (senior year),
Represented 200 seniors.
Led all meetings; parliamentary procedure.

Example of my leadership
Description: *As junior and senior, I served in the student government. Among many responsibilities, I believed we needed a greater interaction with administration and parents.*
Action: *As junior class representative, I asked to serve as the first ever student PTA representative.*
Results: *During my association with the PTA, we initiated first-ever programming for students. The programming provided alternative events (instead of parties). Through these efforts, I was recognized by the Nola High School Board as outstanding junior leader.*
Takeaway: *I believe leadership means involvement and setting a vision among those who are not your peers.*

APPRENTICESHIP

List any of the following creative activities in which you participate or have participated.
1) Drawing
2) Graphic arts
3) Painting
4) Sculpture
5) Photography
6) Other endeavors

High School: (Nola High School)
1) Painting class. Received A. 1999.
2) Photography class. 2000. A-.

College: (Univ. of Elka)
1) Desktop publishing class. A. 2001.
2) Designed a brochure for student activities office. 2002.

List all of the school related activities in which you held a leadership position.

(This may include your high school class, student government, student organizations, clubs, teams within classes, etc.)

High school (Nola High School)
1) Student government. Junior year
2) Senior class president 1999.

College: (Univ. of Elka)
1) Fraternity president. 2001
2) Public Relations Society Secretary. 2002.
3) Account executive in Advertising practicum class. John's Ford was client.

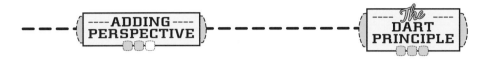

---- ADDING ----
PERSPECTIVE

---- The ----
DART
PRINCIPLE

— APPRENTICESHIP —

Nola University, New Hampshire
Painting class 2003. Received grade of A
Key projects: cubist rendering; classical oil
Sold three projects during fair for over $100
each.
Received two Best in Class awards at school's
art fair

Photography class 2000
A-
Submitted 12 photos included in student
newspaper

Example of my creativity, tenacity, and innovation
Description: *Over the past three years, I have taken art classes and competed in the university's art fair. Additionally, I am financing my way through college.*
Action: *I have won two Best in Class awards due to my paintings of local buildings. In fact, the owners of the buildings have purchased the works for over $100. With this popularity, I started my own business, creating renderings of local buildings and homes.*
Results: *In the past year and a half, I have painted and sold over 20 buildings and homes and have paid entirely for my tuition.*
Takeaway: *I believe that I have leveraged my talents and creativity to meet my goals.*

Account executive in Advertising practicum class
University of Elka, Butler, New Hampshire
Chief contact with client: John's Ford
Developed three advertisements; including one which increased traffic to store 10%
Client personally called instructor to cite group's performance

Example of my persistence, conflict resolution
Description: *One of my advertising practicum classes involves handling a client. My client is a local auto dealership, John's Ford. The client was having difficulty with the local newspaper and their creative staff. Thus, he "hired" me.*
Action: *Unfortunately, I learned the challenge did not lie with the newspaper's staff but with the owner. The owner changed the project's objectives three times during the project. To ensure we had a common agreement, I designed a creative brief for him to approve. The newspaper had never used a creative brief with him before.*
Results: *Once I had approval of the creative brief, I gave it to our creative staff. The staff developed three advertisements which met the owner's goals and were published. The ads increased traffic to his store by 10%. The owner was so pleased that he contacted my instructor and cited the group's efforts.*
Takeaway: *I believe challenges with difficult people can be overcome by establishing agreement among all parties.*

Chapter Summary

Creating Great Narratives Using The DART Principle

Assume the perspective of a great writer.
As you begin to describe your experiences and skills, write a narrative that uses your actual experiences to invoke interest in you.

Use *The College Student's Step-By-Step Guide To Landing A Job*: Dart Principle
The DART Principle provides you with a format to create a concise and compelling narrative about your experiences.

Four major steps comprise the DART Principle:

D: Description. Provide a background of a specific situation where you exhibited or acquired a skill.

A: Action. Describe what specifically you did during this situation.

R: Result. Due to your action, describe the results.

T: Takeaway. Summarize the key point for the interviewer.

You will utilize the DART Principle throughout the remainder of your career preparation process.
Invest the time needed to develop compelling narratives using the DART Principle. Your time will reap benefits throughout the remainder of the career preparation process.

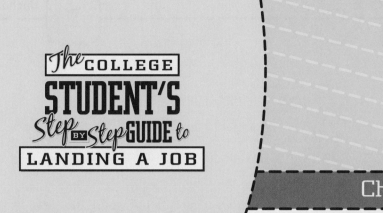

Chapter 6

Insights Into The Buyer Of Your Craft: Employers

By understanding employers' perspectives, you'll help make your career efforts more targeted and more efficient.

Why Am I Doing This?

By now you have written and reviewed your work...endlessly. Frankly, you may be wondering "What does this have to do with resumé writing and job interviewing skills?" So before you begin the next exercise, let's take a reality check.

In the introduction, you received a challenge. Approach the development of your career preparation skills like one of the master creators in our world. Instead of placing your career preparation on your daily "To Do" list, think about creating a masterpiece. Now in the role of the career artisan, you began to uncover your skills and experiences (The Raw Materials Of Your Life), similar to how a sculptor begins to chip away at a piece of marble on the way to creating a work of art.

An employer seeks prospective employees with a collection of specific skills.

But why is uncovering your skills and experiences valuable? Why have you detailed each experience? Why have you noted the smallest aspect of your awards, honors and accolades? As you'll soon learn, employers are seeking a wide variety of skills and experiences, and the sought after skills vary by industry and employer.

An architect interested in bidding for a commission requires a clear understanding of his range, skill and experience. In addition to this basic self-awareness, he must also have insight into the desires of the homeowner. The architect knows he won't win the bid if he pitches a colonial style home to a owner who has her heart set on a Victorian home. Armed with this knowledge, the architect can be sure to bring sketches and examples of his previous work that demonstrates his ability to design charming and attractive Victorian-style homes.

Just as the architect puts much work into preparation for winning the commission on the new home, you have the same type of work ahead of you in your job search.

Your job lies in three areas:
1) Collecting and understanding your skills
2) Researching and understanding the key skills an employer wants
3) Communicating your key skills in a compelling and persuasive manner.

As you are discovering, the process requires a significant investment of time and effort. After all, the employer is going to make a significant investment in you. Thus, you must develop a piece of work (a strong understanding of your skills and values and a method to communicate them) that displays your value and that appeals to the employer.

Let's take a look at a hypothetical situation of a hiring coordinator and her approach to hiring.

Emily M. Ployee, the hiring coordinator of U.R. Dream Company, sits with her colleagues in the company's headquarters. Emily approaches her job in a similar manner as an art collector. Whereas an art collector searches for the inherent value of a piece of art, Emily searches for people who will provide inherent value to her organization.

Today, Emily reviews the list of schools from which her company will recruit during the upcoming year. On the left-hand corner of Emily's desk is a document. Emily calls the document her "Blueprint For Success." Her "Blueprint For Success" displays the essential qualities each prospective candidate must possess in order to become a successful employee.

In Emily's mind, a job is a collection of skills an employee exhibits or performs on an everyday basis. Thus, "The Blue Print For Success" contains a list of highly prized attributes, skills, and characteristics that will make the candidate a successful employee.

> A job is a collection of skills an employee exhibits or performs on an everyday basis.

For instance, Emily often tells her colleagues, "Finance isn't about working with numbers or being able to type balance sheets. Finance is about persistence in examining the financial inputs of an organization and the ability to use critical questioning skills on how the inputs are deployed. Just like engineering is not being able to work with computers, engineering is the ability to be flexible, communicate well, and examine multiple solutions."

In order to hire an applicant, Emily be assured that each prospective employee possesses the needed skills and the ability to communicate those skills and attributes effectively.

But how do you discover the key skill sets Emily seeks? And what skills and experiences are important to the industry and the employers you covet? In the next section, you will learn how to research the skills and experiences employers in your industry seek. You will also find a list of resources available to maximize your researching efficiency.

Chapter Summary

Insights on the Buyer of Your Craft

In the past chapters, you learned about your skills and experiences.
The next step lies in understanding the perspective of the ultimate buyer of your craft, a prospective employer.

Employers believe a job is a collection of skills.
In order to increase your potential for success, you must understand the skills that are most valued by the employers in your industry.

In the upcoming chapters, you will be:
1) Collecting and understanding your skills.
2) Researching and understanding the key skills an employer wants.
3) Communicating the key skills in a compelling and persuasive manner.

Chapter 7

Chiseling Away
To Find The Employer's
Philosophy

The best way to uncover the
key skills that employers covet
is through efficient research.

As you read in the previous chapter, many prospective employers seek specific skill sets. But the question is how do you discover the skills that an employer seeks? What skills and experiences are important to your industry and the employers you covet?

If you were to take a moment and reflect, this step in the career preparation process centers on discovery. Basically, you will be trying to uncover the skills and experiences each of the employers in your industry seeks.

┌─ Learning about key behaviors
└─ that employers value.

And what master creators are better to chisel away at a mass and uncover the beauty of something, but a sculptor? Sculptors purchase a huge mass of stone, metal or other substance and carefully chisel away at it to uncover the true worth of the material. They work diligently to sift through all of the material to expose the most valuable portions of it.

For a career creator such as yourself, you are also given a number of materials, in the form of access to information on employers and industries. And like the sculptor, your challenge lies in uncovering the valuable information and discarding the less relevant portions.

Thus, your goal in this section is to learn how to research the skills and experiences that employers in your industry seek. And as usual, *The College Student's Step-By-Step Guide To Landing A Job* has created a list of resources quickly available to you that will maximize your research efficiency.

How to chisel away at your resources to find what skills and behaviors employers covet.
As you learned in the previous chapter, employers search for key skills and areas of value. Our hypothetical human resources director, Emily, (from the previous chapter) used a checklist of skills, characteristics and behaviors. As you read the passage again, you'll note that Emily is searching for a number of behaviors that indicate the skills a candidate has to offer.

In Emily's mind, a job is a collection of skills an employee exhibits or performs on an everyday basis. "The Blue Print For Success" contains a list of highly prized attributes, skills, and characteristics that will make the candidate a successful employee.

For instance, Emily often tells her colleagues, "Finance isn't about working with numbers or being able to type balance sheets. Finance is about persistence in examining the financial inputs of an organization and the ability to use critical questioning skills on how the inputs are deployed. Just like engineering is not being able to work with computers. Engineering is the ability to be flexible, communicate well, and examine multiple solutions."

In order to hire an applicant, Emily must be assured that each prospective employee possesses the needed skills and the ability to communicate those skills and attributes effectively.

A key to successful career preparation is understanding what key skills the employer is seeking.

Emily and her company are representative of most organizations. Each is searching for key skills and experiences that create value to them. To discover if a candidate possesses these skills, a prospective employer asks questions of the candidate during an interview or searches for the skills and abilities on a resumé.

Thus, it only makes sense to make each prospective employer's job easier for them by including examples of the targeted skills. But how do we do this?

Your first step: Understand and anticipate the attributes targeted by the prospective employer.
The skills sought by employers will differ by organization and industry. Hence, your first step lies in understanding the behaviors that will likely be sought by employers in your desired industry. Luckily, you have a number of resources. As you'll soon learn, finding the information is similar to the work of a sculptor. You set a goal and begin chipping away to expose the key elements that you need.

To begin your study of skill sets needed in your industry:
1) Schedule an appointment with two to three of your instructors. Poll each one on their perception of the key skill sets for your industry of interest. Target two to three hours for this exercise.

2) Spend an hour with your placement officials or make an appointment for an informational interview with alumni working in your field. Provide the alum with the background for your request (i.e. you are preparing for your job search and are interested in understanding the key skill sets employers search for in candidates).

3) Conduct an internet search at a job search site, such as Monster.com or Hotjobs.com. Review numerous postings and digest the respective job descriptions. Note the key skill sets outlined in the listings.

4) Armed with this information, develop a list of the top 10 to 15 skills and attributes identified as being highly valued.

5) Compile this list in your *The College Student's Step-By-Step Guide To Landing A Job*: Career Toolkit.

6) Once you have compiled your list of 10 to 15 skill sets, your goal lies in identifying examples of them. Luckily you have already invested considerable time to your life experiences and skills.

7) Turn to your *The College Student's Step-By-Step Guide To Landing A Job*: Career Toolkit. Review each of your examples in the DART Principle.

8) Write the corresponding skill set(s) by each of your examples.

To make your search more efficient, a list of 12 skill sets and potential questions follows. This list will help you become more familiar with a range of skill sets and the potential definitions of each. The skill sets and questions may not be completely applicable to your industry, but they should provide you with an additional flavor for the behavior-based interview process. You should feel free to modify the skill sets based on your research. An apprenticeship on the following page also provides further direction.

This list is also in *The College Student's Step-By-Step Guide To Landing A Job: Career Toolkit.*

Skill Set: The definition of the skill set in the employer's mind.

Leadership: Key: show facet of leadership

Initiative: Key: Doing something on own; not being requested

Drive, Persistence: Key: Moves forward despite obstacles

Teamwork: Key: Moves team toward goal. Motivates others to contribute synergy; whole greater than sum

Communication Skills: Key: Ability to articulate. Presentation or written skills

Handling Challenges: Key: Overcoming adversity.

Time Management: Key: Prioritize.

Motivation: Key: Enjoy what you do. Gets others to contribute. Challenges both self and others.

Problem Solving: Key: Your approach to tackling challenges.

Conflict Resolution: Key: Listens to others' points of view. Willing to find a mutually winning solution

Innovation: Key: Challenge status quo. Takes risk. Reevaluates current methods.

Analysis: Key: Researches the major reasons why something is occurring. Takes broad quantity of information and examines for trends and implications.

Other Skill Set _____

Other Skill Set _____

Other Skill Set _____

Directions

In this section, you will review the representative list of key skill sets and a brief definition of each. From your research with placement officials, instructors and alumni, circle the key skill sets and definitions for your industry of interest.

Additionally, add any other key skill sets that employers target for your industry under the "Other Skill Set" section.

This section will serve as an ongoing reference for you. As you build your resumé and hone your interviewing skills, you will strive to improve your ability to communicate that you possess the targeted skill sets.

 — Key Skill Sets

APPRENTICESHIP

Problem Solving
Key: Your approach to tackling challenges.

Conflict Resolution
Key: Listens to others' points of view. Willing to find a mutually winning solution.

Innovation
Key: Challenges status quo. Takes risks. Reanalyzes current methods.

Other Skill Set
_____

Other Skill Set
_____

Other Skill Set
_____

APPRENTICESHIP

Directions

Now you possess an understanding of key skill sets. You will take this knowledge and apply it to your *The College Student's Step-By-Step Guide To Landing A Job:* Career Toolkit.

In this exercise, you will move to the DART PRINCIPLE section of your *The College Student's Step-By-Step Guide To Landing A Job:* Career Toolkit. After each example, you will write the key skill set or sets you exhibited by each experience. In some instances, you may be able to place multiple skill sets next to an experience. An example follows.

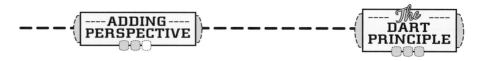

----ADDING----
PERSPECTIVE

The DART PRINCIPLE

Alpha Zi Gamma Sorority volunteer Coordinator; Johnson, Idaho. *Chaired sorority's major volunteer event.* *Served as coordinator: 2003.* *Arranged all logistics; public relations, coordination with American Lung Association.* *200 participants raised $1,000 for American Lung Association.*	*Teamwork* *Communication Skills* *Initiative*
Nola High School, Nola, New Hampshire. *Student Government - 1998 (junior year), Represented 400 students.* *Junior Class Representative.* *Served as representative to PTA; weekly meetings, finance committee.* *Senior Class President - 1999 (senior year), Represented 200 seniors.* *Led all meetings; parliamentary procedure.* *Named outstanding senior leader.*	*Leadership* *Time Management*
Foothills Softball Association, Batter, New Hampshire. *Served as treasurer: 1 year (2003).* *Budget Control; maintained spending, fundraising. Budget: approximately $20,000.* *Key accomplishment: initiated new fund-raiser; $5,000 increase in funds.* *Allowed association to purchase new uniforms.*	*Leadership* *Persistence* *Initiative*

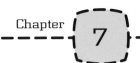

Chapter Summary

Chiseling Away To Find The Employer's Philosophy

Employers believe a job is a collection of skills and experiences an employee demonstrates.
Your goal is to show you possess the skills they need.

The first step is to make the employer's goal easier.
Research the key skills each employer wants. Then make sure you address them in your cover letter, resumé and interview preparation.

Assume the perspective of a sculptor to uncover the key skills an employer seeks.
Learn about the key skill sets through research.
1) Make an appointment with one or more of your instructors and gain their insight.

2) Make an appointment with a placement official.

3) Conduct an informational interview with an alumnus in the industry.

4) Conduct an internet search on recruiting websites.

Develop a list of the targeted 10 - 15 skill sets for your industry.
Be sure to also include a small definition of each skill set.

Identify instances of the skill set in *The College Student's Step-By-Step Guide To Landing A Job*: Career Toolkit.
Once you have identified your 10 – 15 skill sets, write the skill set demonstrated next to each of your examples in the DART Principle. Your example may demonstrate one or a number of skill sets.

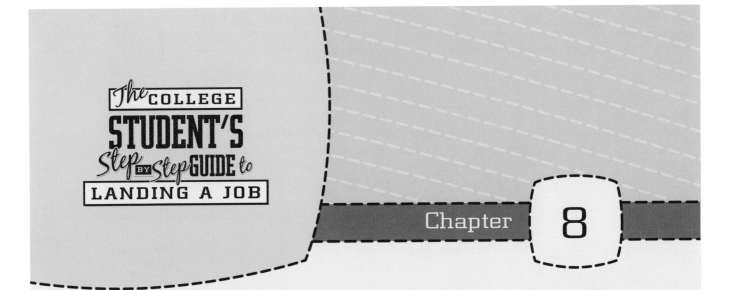

The College STUDENT'S Step by Step GUIDE to LANDING A JOB — Chapter 8

The Difference Between Talent & Genius

Successful career preparation combines an understanding of what you learned in school with the dynamics of the industry in which you are interested.

Have you ever met someone with extraordinary musical talent? He or she may be able to immediately pick up a musical instrument and play it. Or how about the friend who can't read music but can play the piano like it's second nature? That person has a raw talent that either came from genetics or a gift of an intuitive feel for music.

But for all of that talent, your friend maybe plays in a band on the weekends. He or she might make a couple of bucks at local clubs or regional venues. But she hasn't increased her skills for quite some time and doesn't have that special something to take her talent to the next level.

To become proficient during an interview, integrate your academic learning and the actual application of knowledge in your industry.

However, another friend who isn't nearly as musically talented just showed up on MTV. The person played in the high school marching band, was a member of the jazz band and sang in the choir. She never did sit in the first chair, which was reserved for the top musician, and she wasn't always a shoo-in for the honor of solo vocalist. So what's the difference between your two friends? Obviously it's not based solely on pure talent. For some folks, it's dedication that turns raw talent into pure genius.

Success does not always require pure genius or an intuitive gift, it often requires old fashioned hard work and perseverance.

The world's greatest musicians have married their talent with an understanding of their trade and have transformed themselves into geniuses. While Beethoven was unquestionably born with an enormous amount of talent, he also meticulously studied clefs, quarter-notes, staccato and pitch to elevate his ingrained skill into genuine artistry. In order to be perceived by others as truly amazing or valuable, the composer must develop an understanding of his or her trade.

In this same way, you must understand the basic vernacular, trends and expectations in your desired field. Suppose you have two friends, Sam and Jon, who are interested in becoming plumbers. Sam has always been mechanically inclined. He uses his natural talent, combined with a quick trial-and-error strategy as he takes his classes at his vocational technical school. Intuitively, Sam knows how all the parts, pieces and processes should flow together. As a result he is able to finish many projects ahead of his classmates. Sam occasionally has read a few plumbing books and has a rough idea of the jargon used in the plumbing industry. But he feels that as long as it works, why worry about the small details such as the newest techniques and using the exact words for tools. He absolutely loves plumbing because it comes so easily and he is excited about entering the field.

Meanwhile, Jon possesses the same career ambition; however, he's not as mechanically inclined as Sam. Regardless, Jon perseveres. He reads the same plumbing books and he calls the publisher of a few plumbing magazines so he can receive the student rate when he subscribes. He attends a few professional seminars every semester (even though he has to scrimp and save for them) and he subscribes to an e-newsletter that highlights the trends on the plumbing industry. On his breaks from school, Jon makes an extra effort to call a few plumbers and pick their brains about the industry. Jon also diligently sought an internship so he could serve as an apprentice under a master plumber for a few months.

If you are the prospective employer, who will you hire?

Friendships aside, the money is on Jon. He displayed a great deal of initiative and learned about the actual industry. Jon has gained insight through multiple sources, including reading the basic books, subscribing to a few magazines and learning the newest trends. When speaking to an employer, Jon is apt to ask more insightful questions, speak from experience and inquire about current trends. In effect, he has developed a strong link between his academic learning and his actual knowledge about the industry. Jon is more successful...even without the natural talent.

So how do you move beyond raw talent to develop genius? It takes a range of commitment, but the first step lies in truly understanding your industry. In this section you will learn to use your academic training and then add an active knowledge of what really goes on in your industry.

In order to learn your trade:
1) Learn the jargon of your trade.
2) Subscribe to a top magazine in your intended industry.
3) Scan textbooks for relevant insight and information.
4) Ask a professor or an instructor for recent journal articles.
5) Use internet job sites as a source for key skill sets.
6) Conduct an informational interview with alumni.

1) Learn the jargon.
The first key lies in understanding your industry's language. By using the same vocabulary as practicing professionals, you create a perception of knowledge.

Does this matter? Absolutely! Place yourself in the employer's mindset. If a candidate interviewing for a marketing job states, "Yes, my goal is to make kids buy some of my product," the interviewer may question the candidate's true ability, insight and preparation.

However if the next candidate states, "My goal is to provide a compelling reason for my target consumers to increase their buying rate of my product," which candidate would you hire? It's a fair assumption candidate two has done her homework. She took it upon herself to learn about the industry and actually apply her newfound vocabulary when it counts.

2) Subscribe to a top magazine in your industry.
Whether it's the *Chronicle of Higher Education*, *Brandweek*, or *Engineering Today*, pay for a subscription. Most magazines offer a student discount, and it's a small price to pay when you consider it an investment in potential job offers.

If you are on a budget, visit your school library. Skim through each edition and make a copy of any interesting articles. Another option is to visit the magazine's website. The magazine may provide an e-mail update of recent news or trends in the industry. Place the magazine's homepage as the start page of your home computer. Whenever you start cruising the Internet, you'll unavoidably learn a little.

3) Use the BLUEPRINT FOR SUCCESS: INTERVIEW PREPARATION or make a mini-reference booklet.
The BLUEPRINT FOR SUCCESS: INTERVIEW PREPARATION is a guide to help you capture all of the key elements for understanding your industry. The guide provides a quick, concise method to summarize key learning.

The first section outlines the key trends and essential facts about the industry. As you conduct research on your industry, centralize your major learning on this worksheet. The second section outlines the key players in the industry, the competition. Obviously, you need to understand the major players within your industry of interest.

The next section outlines the skill sets the industry targets. As you research job sites, talk with your school's placement officials and interview alumni working in the field. You may want to take notes on the key skill sets in this section.

The final two sections detail key terms you may want to jot down to ensure you understand them as well as any key questions you may want to ask or follow up on.

4) Scan your textbooks.
Be efficient; don't read each mammoth text over again. No one wants to go through that pain. Instead, make a copy of each of the chapter summaries. Place your copies in a three-ring binder for easy reference, a mini reference book, then highlight key information. This mini-book will serve as a quick refresher about your industry.

5) Ask a professor or instructor for a recent journal article.
In many instances, a professor may suggest a particularly good journal or even pass on her latest research project to you. As an additional bonus, it can never hurt to make your professor feel respected in her area of expertise.

6) Find trends by skimming.
By skimming the industry's top magazine, you'll probably notice some of the major trends...almost by accident. Either make a copy of the article and place it in your mini reference book or write down the key trends in a central place, like this book in the BLUEPRINT FOR SUCCESS: INTERVIEW PREPARATION.

7) Use Internet Job websites as a source for key skill sets.
Go straight to the companies that interest you. Many companies offer a career opportunities section on their website. Collect quick, efficient clues by reviewing the job descriptions. Write the key characteristics in the BLUEPRINT FOR SUCCESS: INTERVIEW PREPARATION

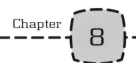

Visit job placement sites, such as hotjobs.com or monster.com. These sites carry a wide array of job listings with job descriptions. Print out applicable job descriptions and begin compiling the skills targeted by employers.

8) **Ask someone who was in your shoes.**
Visit your school's career placement office and ask for the name of an alumni who works in your targeted industry. Call and make an appointment for an informational phone interview with the person.

The interview is simply intended to provide the opportunity to gain information regarding the industry rather than solicit a job interview. Tell the alumni you're preparing for a career in their field and were wondering if they will share career tips with you. Some quick keys to an informational interview follow.

1) Limit the informational interview to 30 minutes.

2) Schedule the interview at the alumni's convenience.

3) Make sure you've prepared a thorough list of questions. Questions may include key traits needed in the industry, major trends, key skill sets, and any other qualities organizations seek in their candidates.

4) Within one day of the informational interview, send a handwritten or typed thank you note to the alumni. Remember, this person has invested time in you. Make a strong effort to truly show your appreciation beyond a simple e-mail.

Remember, the key that sets apart talent from true genius is a level of dedication. While it does mean more work for you, the reward of a job more than pays for the time you invest in this activity. Learn about your trade academically and professionally before you begin interviewing. In doing so, you'll create the potential for greater success.

APPRENTICESHIP

This apprenticeship allows you to review the Blueprint For Success: Interview Preparation. This worksheet is also included in *The College Student's Step-By-Step Guide To Landing A Job:* Career Toolkit. As you scan through various reference materials, this template provides you with an opportunity to summarize your findings about the industry.

The **BLUEPRINT FOR SUCCESS** Interview Preparation

Key trends:
1)

2)

3)

Competition and major players in the industry:
1)

2)

3)

Key products in the industry:
1)

2)

3)

Key skill sets needed in the industry:
1)

2)

3)

Key terms:
1)

2)

3)

Notes and questions:
1)

2)

3)

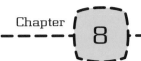

Chapter Summary

The Difference Between Talent And Genius

The difference between raw talent and success:
While individuals with raw talent amaze us every day, it's the true genius who makes an impact on our lives. The difference between an individual with raw talent and the individual who meets with success lies in the each person's respective level of dedication to his passion or vocation.

In order to truly be great at career preparation, you must assume a new level of awareness about your industry. You must truly expand beyond what comes naturally to you and actively delve into the subject to understand what is actually occurring in the industry.

In order to learn your trade, successful career artisans:
1) Learn the jargon of their trade.
2) Subscribe to a top magazine in their intended industry.
3) Scan textbooks for relevant insight and information.
4) Ask a professor or instructor for recent journal articles.
5) Use internet job sites as a source for key skill sets.
6) Conduct an informational interview with alumni.

Best of all, write all of your learning in *The College Student's Step-By-Step Guide To Landing A Job:* Career Toolkit.

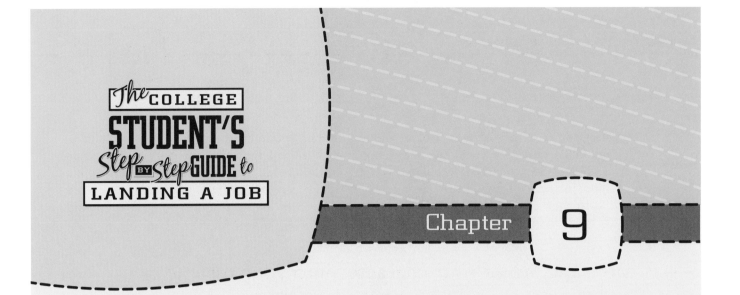

Writing An Award Winning Resumé

Meaningfully differentiate yourself from your competition by transforming your resumé from a list of responsibilities into a representation of you.

Have you ever looked at a piece of art and just become awestruck. Or maybe you've read a book and told someone, "I would love to have a cup of coffee with the author." The piece of art or the book ignited your interest. It captured you in some unique way and you wanted to learn more about the person behind it.

Why? How can someone else create something so stimulating to us?

—— Breathe the fire of your character into your resumé. ————

A great book at its most basic level is a collection of paper and words. However, great authors create masterpieces that express their creativity and themselves. Through talent and hard work, the writer transforms a piece of paper and a mound of verbs, adjectives and nouns from being void of emotion and character into a living form of communication. A great book lives, it involves you, it wants you to savor it, to read it fast, to read it slow and maybe to consume it all at the same time. Its characters live, breathe and represent some aspect of its creator and his thoughts.

Imagine if job candidates embraced a similar perspective when creating their resumés. Would you type a resumé simply listing activities and responsibilities or would you transform your resumé into a narrative, a story that compels someone else to read it?

Take a risk and imagine that your medium is paper and your objective is not to create a resumé. Your goal is to create a living, breathing representation of you. High expectations? Absolutely! But why wouldn't you want your resumé to represent your character, your passion, your value, and most of all, your fire?

> How will your resumé truly stand out from the competition?
>
> Change your mindset. Become an author of an award winning narrative about yourself. Call it, "My Resumé"

You may believe that such a goal is a little silly. But really, the difference between simply making a resumé and actually crafting a resumé which represents you, your story and your character is beyond simple semantics. You are trying to create something meaningful to someone else. How can anyone say a resumé is meaningful if it uses the same language and the same brief descriptions everyone else in the job market uses?

Now, place yourself in the employer's shoes. An employer sees an enormous number of resumés for every position. Your job is to entice the employer so much that she invites you to an interview. How can you differentiate yourself? By being different, by being unique, by being YOURSELF. So why wouldn't you transform your resumé into a living, breathing story about you? Why wouldn't you develop a resumé that is so interesting, the prospective interviewer says, "I need to talk to this person!"

The First Step:

Change your perspective! Don't make a resumé, craft one. Don't type, describe and write. And don't think of yourself as putting together your resumé. It's time to become an award-winning author. And your first writing assignment? Create a living document that REPRESENTS YOU and YOUR VALUE. So How Do You Write An Award Winning Resumé?

So How Do You Write An Award Winning Resumé?

Before you learn the nuts and bolts of a resumé, let's review a few goals for every resumé:

Aesthetics: The layout is graphically appealing and easy to read.

Concise: All words are intentional and not wasted. The candidate minimizes words whenever possible; uses active verbs and never uses personal pronouns.

Transmits: The resumé clearly communicates the job skills the employer seeks.

Crystal-clear: The reader easily understands the resumé, its language and its images. The resumé provides a context for the reader by outlining the background and value of the candidate.

Deliberate: The reader's attention gravitates to the important information.

Ignites Interest: The resumé language is interesting and describes experiences rather than tells about responsibilities. The candidate creates a compelling story of his value. The information is three-dimensional rather than two dimensional.

JON JOBSEEKER

EDUCATION

B.A. Economics and Journalism	**Cum Laude**	**GPA: 3.80**
Stone University, Elle, IA		2004

OCCUPATIONAL EXPERIENCE

Advertising Manager.   *Stone Circular*, **Elle, IA**   2002
Student Newspaper with over $100,000 in annual advertising sales.
Key Accomplishments:
- Increased advertising sales 12% over 1999; increased the client portfolio by 22%.
- Supervised four (4) advertising representatives responsible for all advertising sales.
- Wrote copy for over 1,000 advertisements; designed 200 feature advertisements.
- Received 2000 Best in Class award for three advertisements by National College Newspaper.

Econometric Analyst,   **Northeast Bank**   Summer 2000, 2001
Intern for department responsible for econometric modeling and analysis.
Key Accomplishments:
- Created econometric model for state's agricultural sector. Adopted for continued use and analysis by N.E. bank.
- Received highest performance rating on 2001 and 2002 performance reviews.

RELATED EXPERIENCE

President, Gamma Theta Fraternal Organization   2001
Presided over fraternal organization with 85 members. Increased membership 25%

Student Representative, Stone University   2002
Represented 200 Fine Arts Dept. students. Finance committee chair person with oversight of $100,000.

SELECTED ACTIVITIES AND HONORS

2003 Stone University Outstanding Senior Leader Nominee.
One of 20 nominees selected from entire university senior class.

2003 Public Economics Student Society of America (*Stone University Chapter*)
Outstanding Senior Leadership Award. Sole recipient at university.

2003 Omega Gamma Sigma National Economics Honor Society Inductee.
Induction limited to top seven percent of junior class at Stone University.

1999-2003 Dean's List.
Recognized 9 out of 9 semesters.

INTERESTS

Trivia, participated in strong man contest, avid cook. Enjoy reading and writing.

2611 E. Oriole Street #9 • Jefferson, WI 00001 • jon-jobseeker@landthatjobonline.edu • 001.875.4444

Choosing A Resumé Format

Now that you know the goals of every good resumé, it's time to work on the nuts and bolts in writing an award winning resumé. Throughout your college career, you will probably learn about two major classifications of resumés:

• The chronological resumé
• The subject/functional resumé.

A chronological resumé displays information according to successive time periods. For instance, you would read that a student held an internship in 2001, then a summer job in the field in 2002 and a practicum in 2003. The structure provides an easy-to-follow history for the employer.

A subject or functional resumé organizes the information according to topic or skill set. For instance, the resumé headings may relate to a specific skill or skill sets, such as communication skills; organizational skills; leadership skills, etc. The supporting examples under each heading could have taken place throughout your life and may not necessarily be in chronological order.

What's Preferred? A Modified Chronological Resumé...Dripping With Your Character And Fire. As with any portion of *The College Student's Step-By-Step Guide To Landing A Job* every suggestion and process is open to discussion and is subject to personal preference. But if you are looking for a quick recommendation, *The College Student's Step-By-Step Guide To Landing A Job* has one. Through personal experience and through discussing the topic with professional recruiters and employers, our preference is to START with the format of a chronological resumé. The structure of a chronological resumé has one major advantage. It allows you to show the employer that you continued to develop and to increase your skill set.

However, we're not simply recommending the tried and true chronological resumé. The world has changed. Technology, such as scanners, are now used more often. And screening tools, assessment tests and resumé analysis are being adopted by more companies. But even with all of the changes, the same standard resumé is still used by most college students.

The College Student's Step-By-Step Guide To Landing A Job says, "NO WAY!" You need to modify the chronological resumé so it provides you with an opportunity to breathe life into your resumé. Your goal is to win the Pulitzer Prize of resumé writing. And with a few modifications, you'll find it's pretty easy to craft a resumé that is a living, breathing representation of you.

Resumé Format: Feel free to choose from a wide variety of formats that are available to you.

If you are looking to make the most efficient use of your time, modify one of the templates that Microsoft's WORD application provides you. The majority of formats are aesthetically pleasing and you can add information relatively easy. Keep in mind that it's only an aesthetic template. The layouts, such as the elegant resumé template, look great and provide you with a fantastic guide. However, be sure to change the template's headings and do not fall into the trap of following the format of the information on the templates. Instead, consider incorporating *The College Student's Step-By-Step Guide To Landing A Job* tips in this chapter.

An abbreviated sample of a chronological resumé.

ANNA M. PLOYEE

EDUCATION

B.S. Mass Communication   With Honors   May 2005
GPA: 3.50   Jackson University, Jackson, SC   MCASC Accredited
Work approximately 20 hours per week while attending school.

OCCUPATIONAL EXPERIENCE

Public Relations Intern   *Jackson University Athletic Directors Office*   2003
Intern for Sports Information Director of NCAA division two university.
- Wrote and edited 20 press releases regarding Jackson Univ. Men's Baseball team. Placement of press releases resulted in estimated $100,000 in equivalent advertising.
- Developed Jackson. Univ. Women's Softball program, including all photography, layout and copy writing. Over 20,000 programs printed and distributed.
- Received letter of commendation from Jackson Univ. softball and baseball coaches regarding public relations efforts while assisting in recruiting.

Consumer Electronics Sales   *Big Purchase*   2003, 2004
Salesperson for leading U.S. electronics retailer. Worked 20 hours per week during school year.
- Received top monthly salesperson twice in 24 month time period.
- Received exceeds performance rating on 2003 performance review.

RELATED EXPERIENCE

Public Relations Account Executive   *J.U. PR*   2003, 2004, 2005
Account executive for university public relations agency. Served three clients in Jackson community.
- Led two-person student public relations account team. Served three area businesses with sales ranging from $300,000 to $1,000,000.
- Developed a public relations media event drawing over 3,000 people and increasing daily sales by 20% for client in automotive industry.

SELECTED ACTIVITIES AND HONORS

Member. Public Relations Student Society of America   2002 – 2004
Served on three committees (recruitment, treasury and service).
President. Jackson Domestic Abuse Society   2003 – 2004
- Presided over 100 student and community volunteers.
- Developed shelter's first major fund-raising activity. Adopted as ongoing program.
- Event recognized with "Pride in City" award sponsored by Jackson Mayor's office.

8383 Duke St. • Jackson, SC 00001 • Anna.M@jauno.com • 003.833.0498

Example of Chronological Resumé

ANNA M. PLOYEE

EDUCATION

B.A. English   GPA: 3.00   Jackson University, Jackson, SC   May 2005
Worked approximately 30 hours per week to solely finance education.

OCCUPATIONAL EXPERIENCE

Team Leader   Jack of Burgers   2004
Team leader for quick service restaurant outlet. Responsible for evening shift with crew of eight team members.
- Developed closing procedure checklist, resulting in 50% reduction of Board of Health citations. Checklist implemented by all shifts.
- Served as backup to assistant manager when needed. Provided input into team member performance evaluations. One of two team members possessing key and responsible for closing restaurant.
- Demonstrated consistent high performance resulting in promotion from cashier within 12 months of employment.

Cashier   Jack of Burgers   2003, 2004
Cashier for fastest growing restaurant chain in the state. Worked 30 hours per week during school year.
- Named employee of the month 3 out of 12 months in cashier position.
- Received two "perfect" ratings from "mystery shoppers" (assessing customer experience and service).
- Responsible for front line customer service, including order accuracy and total customer experience.

RELATED EXPERIENCE

Server   Miller Hall, Jackson University   2002, 2003
Cafeteria attendant for university. Work study program participant, earning tuition credit.
- Demonstrated flexibility in rotating positions as needed. Trained in server, cashier and salad bar positions.
- Perfect attendance record for two consecutive semesters.

SELECTED ACTIVITIES AND HONORS

Floor Governor   Miller Hall, Jackson University   2003
- Served on two committees (safety and RA selection committee).
- Represented 20 residents in dormitory policy development.

Dean's List   Jackson University   2002 – 2003
- Achieved grade point average above 3.5 for four semesters between 2002 and 2003.

8383 Duke St. • Jackson, SC 00001 • Anna.M@jauno.com • 003.833.0498

9

The Strategy Behind Crafting A Resumé

In this section, you will learn the key strategies used to write an award-winning *The College Student's Step-By-Step Guide To Landing A Job* resumé.

As you read about the strategies, be sure you have completed the previous exercises in *The College Student's Step-By-Step Guide To Landing A Job*: Career Toolkit. The exercises will serve as an ideal reference about your background, your skills and the skills sought by your industry of interest. Plus all of your hard work on the exercises will make crafting your resumé more efficient and less time consuming because you will actually be applying the resources you already created.

Remember!
Use the information in your The College Student's Step-By-Step Guide To Landing A Job: **Career Toolkit** as your primary resource when you are developing your resumé.

An Outline of the Seven Key Sections of *The College Student's Step-By-Step Guide To Landing A Job*: Award Winning Resumé
You will utilize seven (7) key sections. They are:

- **Education:**
  The critical details of your academic experience and training.

- **Occupational Experience:**
  Experiences relating to the targeted position and/or industry.

- **Related Experience:**
  Other valuable and transferable skills.

- **Selected Activities and Honors:**
  An overview of your accomplishments.

- **Technology:**
  The skills and applications in which you have experience.

- **Key Skills:**
  A synthesis of skills. The true selling section of your resumé.

- **Interests:**
  Interesting information about you which helps stimulate small talk.

Each of the seven key sections are detailed in this chapter. To maximize your efficiency, you may want to develop a rough outline of your resumé as you read the remaining portion of this chapter. A rough outline follows and is also in *The College Student's Step-By-Step Guide To Landing A Job*: Career Toolkit.

APPRENTICESHIP

Your Name:

Education:

Occupational Experience:

Related Experience:

Selected Activities and Honors:

Technology:

Key Skills:

Interests:

Your Contact Information:

Name and Contact Information

Your First Step To Writing *The College Student's Step-By-Step Guide To Landing A Job*: Award Winning Resumé

The first tool you will learn about is the heading of a resume. Your heading should include your basic contact information, including your name, address, phone number and e-mail address.

Tools

While your contact information should be easy to read, minimize the space devoted to your name and contact information. You'll want to devote as much space as possible to your experiences and skills, the real information employers are seeking.

Name

Place the emphasis on your name by treating the text with bold or by maximizing the point size of the text.

Remember to include your e-mail address as well as your full mailing address.

Address

Place the address at either the top or the bottom of the page.

Ensure the address is easy to read, but do not devote a great deal of space on your resumé to your address. The type font size should range between 10 to 12 points for your address and contact information. Consider using a font size ranging from 12 to 36 points for your name.

Find methods to minimize space by stacking your contact information, using a header and footer or placing the contact information to the side of your name.

JON JOB

2611 E. Oriole Street #9
Jefferson, WI 00001
jon-job@fiction.edu
001.875.4444

JON JOB

2611 E. Oriole Street #9 Jefferson, WI 00001 jon-job@fiction.edu 001.875.4444

JON JOB

2611 E. ORIOLE STREET #9 JEFFERSON, WI 00001
001.875.4444
jon-job@fiction.edu

Education Section

Strategy:

The education section is where you detail your academic pedigree. Focus on the key points that relay your value and ignite interest for the employer, such as academic training and your cognitive ability. For instance, highlight your degree or place emphasis on key information, such as if you graduated with honors or if your program was accredited.

Most of all, use the space wisely.

• Minimize the space devoted to your dates of attendance and the location.

• Consider using two to three lines in your education section at the maximum.

• Think about the reader. Emphasize the information that he or she is interested in.

• Place the most important information to the left and the least important information the right.

• Consider placing the most important information in bold, but do not use bold excessively.

B.S. Mechanical Engineering (ESD accredited)   May 2003
80 credit hours in Engineering   University of Elso, Elso, MO

B.A. Counseling and Human Resource Development   August 2001
Cum Laude   South University, Dynamic, IL

B.S. Mass Communication   University of Success, Start, WY
Broadcast emphasis   May 2002

B.S. Physical/Special Education   *GPA: 3.9 on 4.0 scale*   May 2004
Solely financed college education.   Wonder University, Jackson, CA

B.S. English. *Business Communication Emphasis*   May 2004
Political Science Minor.   Lawrence Univ., Jon, OH
Held additional employment (20 hrs. per week during 2000-2004 semesters)

Bachelor of Science. Electrical Engineering   **With Honors**   June 2002
GPA: 3.8 on a 4.0 scale   Part Technical Institute, Jeff, AZ

In this section, you will see the beginning of a resumé. The contact information and the educational section has been applied to a hypothetical student's resumé. As you review the apprenticeship, notice the emphasis focuses on the key information.

JON SUCCESS

EDUCATION

B.S. Physical/Special Education   *Cum Laude*

Wonder Teachers University, Jackson, CA   May 2002

2611 E. ORIOLE STREET #9 JEFFERSON, WI 00001
001.875.4444
jon-success@fiction.edu

JON SUCCESS

2611 E. Oriole Street #9
Jefferson, WI 00001
jon-success@fiction.edu
001.875.4444

EDUCATION

B.S. English   *Business Communication emphasis*   *With Honors*

Wonder Teachers University, Jaac, MO   May 2002

In this example, Jon emphasizes his academic training (through his degree) and his mental horsepower (by noting he graduated cum laude). He also places the most important information in bold text.

In this example, Jon specifies he not only has training in the study of English but that he also specialized in business communication. Finally, Jon emphasizes his cognitive ability by displaying he graduated with honors. Jon could have also highlighted his GPA to reinforce his cognitive abilities.

The Experience Section

Two Key Types of Experiences

In the experience section, you describe your two different types of experiences, your occupational experience and related experiences. Occupational experiences focus directly to the industry and/or position you desire. Related experiences discuss important situations and valuable skills you exhibited and/or developed, but they may not be specifically requested by an employer or they may not be listed on the job description.

Occupational Experience

Occupational experiences are experiences and skills that are job related. As you conducted research on the industry that interests you and by reviewing key job descriptions in employer's ads, you should have already developed a list of key skills your industry or employer wants. Thus, your goal in this section is simple. Show you have had exposure to the industry and displayed the targeted skill sets that the employer seeks.

Occupational Experience:
Examples may include internships, jobs within or related to the industry, practicum classes and even case study experiences.

For instance, if you are applying to an advertising agency as a creative assistant, you may need to demonstrate your ability to visually present information. In this case, examples of occupational experience may include your work study position in which you used a desktop publishing computer application to lay out a flier for your organization's event. In the section, other occupational experiences for college students often occur as a result of internships, previous jobs, class projects or practicums.

To actually develop statements for this section, you will write interesting, intriguing statements regarding your major responsibilities and accomplishments for each position. Luckily, you already accomplished a major portion of this work. In fact, it's time to refer back to *The College Student's Step-By-Step Guide To Landing A Job:* Career Toolkit. As you may remember, in the DART Principle section, you developed a number of statements, that outlined a specific skill set that you have displayed. This is the perfect material to place in your resumé.

The **DART PRINCIPLE**

Example of my initiative and leadership

Description: *For past three years 2001 – 2004, Foothills Softball Association could not afford new uniforms for children 8 – 10. Annual fund-raising efforts had been stalled.*

Action: *As newly installed treasurer, had two goals. Ensure spending is controlled and initiate fund-raising efforts. Enlisted 12 volunteers, 4 local businesses and all participants. Ensured collaboration of entire committee. Initiated new fund-raising effort.*

Results: *Fund-raiser netted $5,000 and allowed uniform purchases. Largest fund-raiser in history of association. Received letter of commendation from association president.*

Takeaway: *I believe a strong key to leadership is initiative as well as collaboration. This example displays my type of leadership.*

The **Description** section provides you with the information you will need for each heading, such as the company or association, your position and the dates.

The **Action and Results** sections provides you the information about your responsibilities and the impact you made in each position and organization.

In your resumé, you will summarize this information into a tightly packed, interesting format for the reader.

70

The following examples are designed to provide you with guidance on how to structure the occupational experience statement. Please note, you have already accomplished the majority of this work in THE DART Principle section. As you read, you should be able to maximize your efficiency by again drawing upon the A, (action) and R, (result section).

OCCUPATIONAL EXPERIENCE

- Managed organizational marketing budget exceeding $25,000 and met all budgeting objectives.

- Trained over 30 conference volunteers; received an overall rating of 4.8 on 5.0 scale from training attendees.

- Increased membership into fraternity by 25% in one year. Maintained 100% retention of new members over two-year period.

- Wrote Eppa University Economic Society's first vision statement. National organization uses statement as preferred template for all U.S. societies.

- Wrote, designed and coordinated first direct mail campaign targeting alumni for university's psychology department. Campaign resulted in $10,000 in donations. Largest campaign in fraternity's history.

- Exceeded sales hurdle for four consecutive months. Assigned to mentor new employees during new hire probationary period.

- Served as business counselor for over 20 entrepreneurs at the University of Stone's Small Business Development Center.

- Taught three sections of English to 60 high school students. Received a 9.0 on a 10.0 scale for overall teaching effectiveness from students.

- Served as play-by-play sports announcer for 20 football games televised to over 2,000 university students via student television station.

- Wrote copy for four press releases for John's in Greece restaurant. Press releases published by four newspapers with 50,000 in paid circulation. Free publicity estimated at $10,000.

- Developed daily summer teaching plan for child care center. Curriculum implemented center-wide.

-- APPRENTICESHIP --

Related Experience

The related experience section provides an overview of your other valuable skill sets, which may be secondary for an employer. Related experience examples often emanate from your work in classes, groups for classes, seminars, volunteer positions, professional development associations and extracurricular activities.

Let's think of a hypothetical example of a local newspaper who seeks a candidate for its advertising department. The classified ad communicates a need for writing, photography and layout skills. However, you know from your research, the other needed skills in the industry include initiative, teamwork and leadership. To tout your leadership skills, you include your experience with student government .

President	Stone University Economics Fraternity.	2003 – 2005
Presided over 100 student members and budget exceeding $12,000.		

You also develop a compelling narrative on your resumé regarding the teamwork skills that you demonstrated when you served as the weekend manager of a fast food restaurant and supervised nine other employees.

Daypart Manager	Eat At Joe's Diner, Jackson, NM	2004 – 2006
Supervision of 9 employees; scheduling weekly shifts for all team members; developing evaluations.		

And your initiative is demonstrated when you describe the fund-raising program you developed for your sorority or fraternity. All of this experience would be communicated in your related experience statements.

Fundraising Chairperson	Laure Elpha Sorority	2004 – 2006
Developed three fundraising projects that raised over $2,000; highest amount in sorority history.		

A few examples of related experience statements follow on this page and the upcoming apprenticeship. Remember, the related skills section outlines valuable skills that may not be directly requested for the position.

Manager, Advertising Class	389: Advertising Campaign	Fall 2005
Led five member student team to develop a marketing and promotional communication plan. (A project). Designed a multimedia advertising campaign, including print, television and internet advertising (BMW).		
Training Assistant	Jackson Bank, Jackson, MO	2003 – 2005
Over two-year period, trained 49 new employees on company's security and financial procedures.		

In this apprenticeship, you will review examples of statements that are intended to be placed in the related experience section of your resumé.

The related experience section contains examples of experiences that show you possess key skills or traits. While the job description may not specifically ask for the skill set, your research indicates they are universal. For instance, your leadership ability may have allowed you to become student government vice president or you displayed your communication skills by serving as a tour guide for the admissions office. Remember to use *The College Student's Step-By-Step Guide To Landing A Job: Career Toolkit* as a reference for this information, utilize the DART Principle section. The action and result section should provide you with the key elements to include in your related experience section.

-- APPRENTICESHIP --

RELATED EXPERIENCE

President. Stone University Economics Fraternity.
Presided over 100 student members and budget exceeding $50,000. (2003 - 2005)

Conference Attendee. National Conference of University Leaders. Jan. 2005
One of 100 delegates chosen from national pool of college students.

Volunteer Coordinator. Land Univ. Cancer Society Marathon. 2005
Led recruitment of 22 volunteers for event with 1,000 participants and $12,000 donated. Largest number of participants in event's history.

Director. Success Univ. Men's Softball Intramural League. 2003
Coordination, recruitment, scheduling of 20 men's teams, 200 participants.

Multilingual: Fluent in French language. Over 18 collegiate hours in French language.

Volunteer Speaker. "School is Fun" Reading Program. Jay, MO Fall 2003
Presented and spoke to 12 classes regarding importance of education (Johnson Elementary, Johnson, WV)

Volunteer Team Leader. Land University Cancer Association. Spring 2005
Led team of 12 individuals in raising over $200 for charity.

Vice President. Students Against Drunk Driving. 2002 – 2003
Responsible for developing SADD presentation for all incoming freshmen class members. Obtained signed contracts from 15% of class.

Volunteer. Special Olympics, Jackson, NM 2003
Coordinated state wide bowling tournament and awards banquet. Acquired donations to provide 300 participants with prizes at no cost to organization.

Writing The Occupational Experience and Related Experience Sections

First, begin with your rough outline of your resumé. By this time, you have already jotted down the information for your education and roughed out your name and contact information. Now it's time to begin placing your occupational and related experiences in chronological order beginning with the most recent one.

Remember, space on your resumé is precious. Your goal is to maximize every word available and help the employer understand why working with a specific organization, industry or firm was important.

Start with the headings.
Your first task in each of the sections is to write a rock-solid headline. As in newspaper writing, you will want to provide the most important information at the beginning. This information includes the place, location and position that comprise each of your experiences. Begin with the title you held during the experience.

Next, provide the reader with a perspective of the organization. For instance, summarize what industry the organization participates in, the size of the organization, its revenues or some other metric. ***Ideally, you want to tell the employer why working for the organization was valuable.*** Finally, identify the time of employment with the organization. Remember, this is the least important of the information, so maintain it on the far right side of the paper.

Use *The College Student's Step-By-Step Guide To Landing A Job:* Career Toolkit as a reference. The Description section should provide you with the organization or activity's name, date and location as well as your position.

Publishing Intern Baxter Publishing   Jan. – May 2005
Intern for fourth largest publishing company in U.S., Baxter Publishing, Tor WA

Administrative Assistant.   **University of Illa**   Jan 2001 – Sept. 2003
Work Study for Univ. of Illa Admission Department. Department schedules over 10,000 visits.

Weekend Grocery Manager   Summer 2003, 2004
Flowers Food Center. Regional chain with 2 outlets and $4,000,000 in sales.

Student Representative. University of Success Student Government.
Represented 400 students in university Fine Arts department.   2003 - 2005

Treasurer, Alpha Phi Omega Fraternity.   Sand University   2003
Controlled a budget exceeding $50,000 for organization with 100 members.

Advertising Copywriter, Student Tribute   2001 - 2003
Copywriter for student newspaper with 10,000 circulation and 38 editions per year.

Writing Statements

Now that you know the type of information to include in the headings and statements for your occupational and related experiences, let's discuss the method to make each statement as compelling as possible. As an award winning resumé author, you goal is to ignite interest in the employer. Remember, the employer has no idea who you are nor what you are. This is your first opportunity to truly generate interest in the employer and be invited for an interview. Thus your resumé must move beyond a representation of you and your skills and actually represent your accomplishments. And on top of all of this information, your resumé must represent your passion for the company and the industry by using strong, vivid descriptions about you, your accomplishments and skills.

Don't allow yourself to fall into the trap of placing only responsibilities under each heading. Show how you made an impact. And remember, *The College Student's Step-By-Step Guide To Landing A Job:* Career Toolkit is the collection for all of your incredible skills, accomplishments and impact. As you review the apprenticeships and begin to develop your own occupational and related experience statements, remember great statements for each of the two sections should possess seven key elements.

Focus on describing results and accomplishments. You want to convey to the reader that you have the skills they are seeking. The best method is to describe them by using the information you wrote in the A and R section of the DART principle.

Quantify and qualify. Move beyond simply listing responsibilities. As suggested earlier, provide a three-dimensional description of your history. For instance, quantify results when possible or show that a project you initiated has continued.

Be as specific as possible. Get straight to the point in as few words as possible.

Be concise. Remove non-value added words such as: a, an, the, this, that, which, can, will, etc.

Use active verbs. Avoid is, was, were, have, had. Instead use active verbs to describe your skills and accomplishments.

Write a compelling story. Structure your statements to tell a story about your skills and accomplishments. Again, use the A and R section of the DART principle in your stories.

Keep the reader in mind: In detailing and framing your experiences, keep in mind the key skills targeted by employers in your industry. Again, reference your research in *The College Student's Step-By-Step Guide To Landing A Job:* Career Toolkit.

Creating Statements

In this apprenticeship, you are provided with an example of a DART Principle and then the transformation into a occupational and related experience statement. As you will notice, the statements are concise and rely heavily on the information in the A (action) and R (result) section.

Example of my initiative and leadership

Description: *For past three years 2001 - 2004, Foothills Softball Association could not afford new uniforms for children 8-10. Annual fund-raising efforts had been stalled.*

Action: *As newly installed treasurer, had two goals. Ensure spending is controlled and initiate fund-raising efforts. Enlisted 12 volunteers, 4 local businesses and all participants. Ensured collaboration of entire committee. Initiated new fund-raising effort.*

Results: *Fund-raiser netted $5,000 in funds and allowed uniform purchases. Largest fund-raiser in history of association. Received letter of commendation from association president.*

Takeaway: *I believe a strong key to leadership is initiative as well as collaboration. This example displays my type of leadership.*

Transform your Action and Result section into strong statements about the impact you made.

Under the heading, you may want to write:

Developed largest fund raising event in history of organization.

Recognized for leadership in letter of accommodation from association president for exceeding expectations for fund-raising event.

The most compelling statements on your resumé use active verbs and strong nouns. Active verbs create imagery and assist in communicating your value. Strong nouns provide context for the reader. To assist you in writing your resumé statements, a list with a host of active verbs and strong nouns follows.

Actions

Awarded	Developed	Implemented	Produced
Championed	Established	Increased	Ranked
Changed	Evaluated	Initiated	Recognized
Created	Exceeded	Integrated	Recommended
Decreased	Fund raising	Led	Researched
Defined	Garnered	Managed	Responsible for
Demonstrated	Generated	Oversaw	Rewarded
Designed	Impacted	Owned	Supervised

Nouns

Bottom Line	Finance	Net Revenues	Sales
Budget	Gross Revenues	Percent	Savings
Channels	Incremental	Portfolio	Strategy
Costs	Margin	Proficient	Taskforce
Distribution	Marketing	Profit	Team
Employees	Media	Project	Top line
Expenses	Multifunctional	Recipient	Value

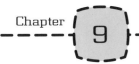

Selected Honors And Activities Statement

In the next section of your award winning resumé, you will detail select honors and activities that you believe are valuable. In this section, your goal is describe to the employer that your skills and abilities have been validated. In essence, you are using a third party to provide credibility to your skills, abilities and accomplishments.

Many college students use this section to display key characteristics, such as their cognitive ability by describing that they were awarded a scholarship or were inducted into an honor society.

Additional examples of select honors and activities may come from extracurricular activities and organizations, part-time and/or summer jobs, seminars, competitions, honor societies, professional development organizations, standardized test scores and creative talents.

Keys to great statements:
- Each statement should help describe to the employer one of your key skills, traits or abilities.
- You should provide enough description in each statement and heading to allow anyone to totally understand your affiliation, honor or participation. Don't forget to include the details of the honor, who it was from, why and where. Your statement should convey enough information to make it self-explanatory.

University of Success Outstanding Senior Leadership Award, 2003: One of 10 university-wide nominees and recipients.

Sole Recipient of University Mass Communication Superior Scholarship Award (2003)

Cognitive Ability: Score of 34 on ACT. Scored in top 10% of all national students (2003)

Award Winner: Jackson's Barbecue: Recognized as employee of month for two months in a 12 month period. Recognized for ability to up-sell 30% of all customers with 0% complaints in a 30-day period.

Omnicron Delta International Engineering Honor Society: Only 12% of all junior engineering majors inducted.

Creative talent: Wrote and choreographed skit for student talent competition for group winning second place. IU Sing, 2004.

Published writer: Avid poet, published two pieces in local periodical with monthly circulation of 150,000.

Participated in national speech meet: Won second place at state meet to gain invitation to participate at national level. One of 30 students to compete in national event.

Recognized for Volunteer Activity: Allen County SPCA
Honored for initiatives to recruit dog walkers from local retirement communities and posting animal adoption posters at local retailers.

Key Skill Sets Section

In the key skill sets section, you provide a three to five bullet point summary of your major benefits to the employer.

This section will probably be quite controversial for most college students.
Many career professionals will debate this section. However, *The College Student's Step-By-Step Guide To Landing A Job:* Key Skill Set section is essential to selling you. This section provides a concise, comprehensive summary of your skills. This is truly the section in which you describe your key skill sets and explain why they are important.

The reason for *The College Student's Step-By-Step Guide To Landing A Job:* Key Skill Set section is simple. If you truly are an award winning resumé writer, why wouldn't you mirror the great authors of our time? Would Steinbeck or Dickens allow someone to describe their own characters? Then, why would you make the reader go to all of the work to characterize you?

What should be included?
This section should not be redundant. It should not be a cut and paste from an earlier section. Instead, each bullet point in the key skill set section should summarize and synthesize two to three major points in your resumé. This can be either academic or applied experience. The key skill set section implicitly states, "Because of this experience, these demonstrated skills and this experience, I possess _____."

How the Key Skill Set Section Should Work
First, the reader scans your resumé for your education and key experiences. She notes a number of key skills and experiences from your Occupational and Related Experience sections. She is gaining a strong sense about you. However, she is crafting a perception about you. As an award winning author, you want to help her develop this perception. You want to ensure what you believe makes you unique for the job is understood by the employer.

Now, the Key Skill Set Section provides three to five benefits of you, your uniqueness and your skills. This section specifically describes how you meet the employer's needs and how you attained this skill. As you read the following example, review how the student summarized his academic and actual experience in the public relations field. Notice, the formula used before, "Because of this experience, these demonstrated skills and this experience, I possess _____."

> **Possess academic and actual experience in public relations:** 18 undergraduate hours in public relations and over 1,000 internship hours with University Sports Information Director's Office.

In this example, the student is submitting her benefits in easy-to-understand, bite-sized pieces to the employer. The key selling point is not the 18 credit hours nor the internship, the key selling benefit is that the student possesses academic and actual experience in her chosen field. Notice how the student first states her benefit and then explains her rationale (i.e. the reason she has experience in public relations is due to her college coursework as well as her internship).

The Formula

In writing the key skills section:

1) Begin with the key benefit or skill you possess. For instance, is it proven sales experience, demonstrated leadership and teamwork or a strong record of analytical skills?

2) Next explain how you developed this key skill. In one to two brief sentences describe the experiences, courses and accommodations which lead you to believe you possess these skills.

3) You should have at least two reasons that describe why you possess this skill.

-- APPRENTICESHIP --

KEY SKILLS

Possess academic and actual experience in public relations: 18 undergraduate hours in public relations and over 1000 internship hours with University Sports Information Director's Office.

Proven sales experience: Two years direct to consumer sales at national retail outlet. Received highest sales performance award given at the outlet.

Ability to multi-task and meet deadlines and priorities: Worked over 20 hours per week to solely finance education. Able to maintain A- average with full academic course load and responsibilities for employment and internship.

Demonstrated leadership and teamwork: Led two-person student team for three years and community volunteer organization for one year. Maintained strong teams and received strong results.

Recognized record of initiative and motivation: Received commendations from municipality and key clients for leadership of community service organization and student public relations team.

Possess strong record of analytical skills: Over 26 credit hours in statistics, finance and macroeconomics and an exceeds rating on the analytical skill section of intern performance review.

Demonstrated conflict resolution abilities: Received A grade in two conflict management classes, Getting to Yes and Advanced Negotiations. Developed skills during organizational behavior internship by facilitating Dynamic Team seminar.

Displayed drive and persistence skills: Self-funded 100% of all college expenses by working 40 hours per week, taking a minimum of 12 credit hours per semester. Finished in five years with B+ average and two internship experiences.

APPRENTICESHIP

Keys To Writing Strong Key Skill Set Statements

Always start with a strong, action verb. Action verbs describe and create an image in the employer's mind.

Summarize. You must condense a number of points in your resumé into each statement. If you decide to cut and paste a sentence into the section, your resumé will become redundant and the employer will potentially dismiss your resumé.

Be as specific as possible. Get straight to the point in as few words as possible.

Be concise. Remove non-value added words such as: a, an, the, this, that, which, can, will, etc.

Write a compelling BENEFIT.
1) Your benefit must be meaningful to the employer.
2) Your benefit must be followed with an explanation of one to two sentences.

You must explain why you believe you possess this skill set.

Other Benefits For The Key Skills Section

Readily accept responsibility

Record of academic achievement

Demonstrated initiative

Accomplished pianist

Demonstrated teamwork

Experienced mentor

Performance and results driven

Proficient with emerging technology

Proven salesperson

Record of strong achievement

Proven self starter

Recognized for performance

Readily accept multiple responsibilities

Strong understanding of and exposure to industry

Dedication to continuing learning

Willingly expand realm of responsibility

History of advancement

Experienced facilitator

Solid professionalism

Proven multi-tasking ability

Demonstrated flexibility

Technology Section

Today, society and organizations are driven by technology and the productivity/value creation ability of their employees. Your goal is to provide a brief overview of your technology skills, regardless of the position you are seeking.

The key to the Technology section:

This section's goal is to provide a high-level overview of your technology skills. To achieve this goal, you should highlight:

• Software applications which you have been exposed to or have experience with

• Programming languages with which you are proficient

• Special hardware or other technology skills

Please remember:

Many employers may not be familiar with a technology or computer application specific to an industry. In order to fully communicate this experience, you may need to provide a brief description of the software.

Examples of Technology Statements

TECHNOLOGY

Proficient with the following computer applications:
• Microsoft Word, Excel, Access and PowerPoint
• Adobe InDesign and Illustrator
• SAS and SPSS
• AutoCAD/AutoCAM

Proficient with the following programming languages:
• C++
• HTML

Experienced with the use of IBM PC/and APPLE platforms and software applications: Word, Excel and PowerPoint, PageMaker, QuarkXpress.

Microsoft certified technician

Certified in diesel mechanic diagnostics

Experience with Health$ell, a healthcare industry marketing database

-- APPRENTICESHIP --

Interest Section

The interest section should always end your resumé. The section serves two purposes. First, the section provides a brief overview of you as a person, listing a few key unique interests. Second, the section provides the inexperienced or experienced interviewer with an opportunity for small talk. The interviewer can use the information to start a brief introductory conversation.

Keys to the Interest Section:

- **Limit the section to one line.**
  Remember, this section encourages small talk; it should not detract from the core of your resumé.

- **Write elements that differentiate you from others.**

- **Omit anything personal and keep a positive tone.**
  An employer does not want to know your weight, height, gender, church affiliation, etc.

- **The unique elements do not have to be earth shattering.**
  No one expects you to conduct experiments with Plutonium. However, perhaps you had a brief claim to fame, collect something unique or have a hobby.

Examples of Statements In Interest Section

INTERESTS

Enjoy cooking. Attended two Chili cookoffs.

1993 Butte County Blue Ribbon Winner. Avid collector of movie posters.

Former radio announcer. Enjoy writing. Goal to read all Steinbeck novels.

Classic auto restorer. Largest penny collection in Wisconsin.

Met 20 celebrities. Volunteer of Make A Wish Foundation.

-- APPRENTICESHIP --

How Should *The College Student's Step-by-Step Guide to Landing a Job* Resumé Look?

After you've devoted the time to preparation, don't lose sight of the details as well. The following tips discuss the aesthetic details to ensure your resumé reflects professionalism and value:

DO remember to incorporate the seven key sections to the resumé.

DO remember to incorporate key headings to provide the reader background.

DO remember to make your resumé aesthetically pleasing.

DO purchase a nine inch by twelve inch envelope. Mail your resumé flat to reduce any folds. (This means you'll need to invest a little extra in postage, but it's worth it.) **DON'T** fold your resumé into a business sized envelope.

> Aesthetics go a long way in projecting your value to the employer. Take care to ensure you've paid attention to the details.

DO deliver your label-addressed envelope directly to the post office to ensure it has the correct amount of postage. Imagine the impression your envelope would make if it arrives "postage due" at the company you covet.

DO use white or neutral paper; it's easier for an employer to make copies and distribute your resumé to others. **DON'T** exhibit your creativity via a neon, pastel or dark paper stock.

DO choose a watermark or high quality resumé paper. Show your attention to detail by using a quality paper. **DON'T** use regular copy paper.

DO use the envelope wizard to print directly on the envelope. Labels lack individuality and can give the perception of being part of a mass mailing. **DON'T** practice your handwriting on the resumé envelope.

DO spend time looking for spelling, grammar, or spacing errors. DON'T review your resumé quickly just to get it out the door. Ask others to review your resumé for errors. Double and triple check before you send your resumé.

DO review your resumé to ensure you have incorporated all of the key skills the employer seeks on your resumé. You have conducted a great deal of research identifying the key skill sets in your industry. You have sought information from a range of sources, including professors, placement officials and alumni. Make sure you maximize your research and cover the needed skill sets in your resumé.

DO review the sample resumé and the sample resumé template on the following pages. Each example should provide you with a strong reference as you write your award winning resumé.

JOE M. PLOYEE

EDUCATION

B.S. Mass Communication
GPA: 3.20

MCASC Accredited
Jackson University, Jackson, SC

May 2005

OCCUPATIONAL EXPERIENCE

Public Relations Intern   **Jackson University Athletic Directors Office**   2003
Intern for Sports Information Director of NCAA Division Two University.
Key Accomplishments:
• Wrote and edited 20 press releases regarding Jackson Univ. Men's Baseball team. Placement of press releases resulted in estimated $100,000 in equivalent advertising.
• Developed Jackson. Univ. Women's Softball program, including all photography, layout and copy writing. Over 20,000 programs printed and distributed.
• Received letter of commendation from Jackson Univ. softball and baseball coaches regarding public relations efforts assisting in recruiting efforts.

Consumer Electronics Sales   **Big Purchase**   2003, 2004
Salesperson for leading electronics retailer. Worked 20 hours per week during school year.
Key Accomplishments:
• Received top monthly salesperson twice in 24 month period.
• Received exceeds performance rating on 2003 performance review.

RELATED EXPERIENCE

Public Relations Account Executive   **J.U. PR**   2003, 2004, 2005
Account executive for university public relations agency. Served three clients.
Key Accomplishments:
• Led two-person student account team. Served three area businesses with sales ranging from $300,000 to $1,000,000.
• Developed a public relations media event drawing over 3,000 people and increasing day's sales by 20%.

SELECTED ACTIVITIES AND HONORS

Member. Public Relations Student Society of America   2002 – 2004
Served on three committees (recruitment, treasury and service).

President. Jackson Domestic Abuse Society   2003 – 2004
• Presided over 100 student and community volunteers.
• Developed shelter's first major fund-raising activity. Adopted as ongoing program.
• Event recognized with "Pride in City" award sponsored by Jackson Mayor's office.

8383 Duke St. • Jackson, SC 00001 • Joe.M@fiction.com • 003.833.0498

JOE M. PLOYEE

KEY SKILLS

Academic and actual experience in public relations: 18 undergraduate hours in public relations and over 1000 internship hours with University Sports Information Director's Office.

Proven sales experience: Two years of direct to consumer sales at national retail outlet. Received highest sales performance award given at the outlet.

Ability to multi-task and meet deadlines and priorities: Worked over 20 hours per week to solely finance education. Able to maintain A- average with full academic course load and responsibilities for employment and internship.

Demonstrated leadership and teamwork: Led a two-person student team for three years and a community volunteer organization for one year. Maintained strong teams and received strong results.

Recognized record of initiative and motivation: Received commendations from municipality and key clients for leadership of community service organization and student public relations team.

TECHNOLOGY

Proficient with the following computer applications:
• Microsoft Word, Excel, Access and PowerPoint
• Adobe InDesign and Illustrator
• SAS and SPSS

INTERESTS

Enjoy music. Avid collector of vinyl records. Completed six marathons. Love to read.

8383 Duke St. • Jackson, SC 00001 • Joe.M@fiction.com • 003.833.0498

JOE M. PLOYEE TEMPLATE

EDUCATION

Your Degree (Bachelor of Arts in Elementary Education)   *Your university*   *City, State*
GPA; Honors   School Accreditation   Graduation Date
Did you self finance education or how many hours per week did you work.

OCCUPATIONAL EXPERIENCE

Your Title   **Company Name and Location**   Date
Background of company. Provide the reader with a context of the business.
- Provided customer service: Notice how the bolded section is the key skill. The most important information belongs on the left side of the paper. Less important information belongs on the right side of the paper.
- Continue to use your examples. Simply tighten the language when possible (i.e. use active wording, especially in the phrases at the beginning). Strive for two sentences or fewer per bullet.
- Provided customer service: Responsible for assisting with client questions and solving client problems (via phone, e-mail and in person) for the finance department.

Marketing Assistant   **Jackson Carnivals, Jackson, WY**   6/2003 – 12/2005
Background of Jackson Carnivals. Provide the reader with a context of the business.
- Design and created marketing materials: Designed marketing materials including promotional flyers, print advertisements and brochures targeted to three business segments.
- Continue to use your examples. Tighten the language when possible (i.e. use very active wording, especially in the phrases at the beginning). Strive for two sentences or fewer per bullet).

RELATED EXPERIENCE

President   **Stone University Economics Fraternity**   10/2003 – 12/2005
Presided over 100 student members and budget exceeding $50,000.

Conference Attendee   **National Conference of University Leaders**   10/2003
One of 100 delegates chosen from national pool. (2004)

8383 Duke St. • Jackson, SC 00001 • Joe.M@fiction.com • 003.833.0498

Use *The College Student's Step-By-Step Guide To Landing A Job*: Career Toolkit.
Remember to use the DART Principle section from your *The College Student's Step-By-Step Guide To Landing A Job: Career Toolkit* for your resumé. Your statements should include the R and the T Section.

JOE M. PLOYEE TEMPLATE

SELECTED HONORS AND AWARDS

Award Winner: Jackson's Barbecue   6/2003
Recognized as employee of month for two months in a 12 month period. Recognized for ability to up-sell 30% of all customers and 0% complaints in a 30 day period.

Omnicron Delta International Engineering Honor Society:
Only 12% of all junior engineering majors inducted.

TECHNOLOGY

Proficient with multiple computer applications:
- **Microsoft Applications:** Microsoft Word, Microsoft Excel, Microsoft PowerPoint, Microsoft Access, Microsoft Outlook, Microsoft Works
- **Website Development:** Microsoft FrontPage
- **Database Applications:** Filemaker Pro Databases,
- **Desktop Publishing:** Quark Express, Adobe Illustrator, Print Shop

KEY SKILLS

Possess academic and actual experience in public relations: 18 undergraduate hours in public relations and over 1,000 internship hours with University Sports Information Director's Office.

Proven sales experience: Two years direct-to-consumer sales at national retail outlet. Received highest sales performance award given at the outlet.

Remember, in this section attempt to combine two or three experiences into a summary.

OTHER INTERESTS

- Provide one to two bullets on some interests. The key is to provide an interesting or unique conversation starter (but not provide in-depth personal information). For instance:
- Avid chili cook, enjoy reading, long to travel to the Scandinavian countries.

8383 Duke St. • Jackson, SC 00001 • Joe.M@fiction.com • 003.833.0498

A Scannable Resumé

Due to the growth of the Internet, electronic communication and the need to realize cost efficiencies, scanning resumés has become a necessity to evaluate prospective employees.

Human Resource Directors and employers use scannable resumés for preliminary resumé sorting. This means resumés will be scanned and a computer will use a software application to conduct the preliminary evaluation of job candidates.

Once your initial resumé is developed and polished, you will need to create a scannable version. Your goal is to produce a resumé format that eliminates design fluff but still is a fire-breathing resumé that captures employers' attention.

Here are some tips to designing a scannable resumé: Eliminate graphics - remove lines, bullets, and other design elements that can distract the reader (and often do not scan in well).

Limit the use of italics, bold, or other accents, as they may not scan well.

Use a basic font (i.e. arial) in your resumé.

Review your resumé and compare it to the employer's job description. Do your resumé and the job description have the same language and key skill sets?

Keep in mind the scanner is seeking specific skills and words, so language is extremely important. Thus, your research on the company and industry will become even more important. Continue to be selective and maximize each word. Work diligently on your resumé and show how your skills align with skills targeted by the employer.

Chapter Summary

Crafting Your Resumé

Transform your resumé from a piece of paper to a true reflection of your character.
Great authors create masterpieces that express their creativity and themselves. Through talent and hard work, the writer transforms a piece of paper and a mound of verbs, adjectives and nouns from being void of emotion and character into a living stet form of communication. Your goal is to transform your resumé into a representation of you.

A fire-breathing resumé is judged in five (5) key areas.
- **Easy:** Graphically appealing and easy-to-read.
- **Concise:** Intentional, precise wording.
- **Crystal clear:** Outlines the candidate's background and value.
- **Ignites interest:** Describes the candidate's value rather than lists responsibilities.
- **Transmits:** Clearly communicates the candidate possesses the targeted skills.

The College Student's Step-By-Step Guide To Landing A Job Award Winning Resumé contains seven (7) elements.
- **Education:** The critical details of your academic pedigree.
- **Occupational Experience:** Experiences relating to the targeted position and/or industry.
- **Related Experience:** Other valuable and transferable skills.
- **Selected Activities and Honors:** An overview of your accomplishments.
- **Technology:** The skills and applications in which you have experience.
- **Key Skills:** A synthesis of multiple skills and experiences. The true selling section.
- **Interests:** Interesting or unique information about you that is intended to help start small talk for an inexperienced interviewer.

Utilize The College Student's Step-By-Step Guide To Landing A Job: Career Toolkit as a reference on what to write in your resumé.

Chapter 10

Writing An Award Winning Cover Letter

Create a positive first impression in writing by learning the proper method to develop a great cover letter.

Crafting a Cover Letter

First impressions are important. Imagine a builder who has spared no expense inside the house. He has taken great care to integrate the most desired amenities and details to his model home. He has added cherry cabinetry, slate floors, state-of-the-art appliances and granite countertops. Unfortunately the radiant in-floor heating, cedar closets and ceramic master bath with steam shower depleted the total building budget. So the outside of the house is without grass, landscaping and siding. The buyer pulls into the gravel driveway and tells the realtor, "I'm pretty hesitant on this one. It just doesn't seem right." The realtor smiles and says, "But take a look on the inside. You'll be surprised. It has a lot to offer."

> Your cover letter creates a first impression to the employer. You won't be able to stun them with your new suit unless your cover letter passes the bar.

The buyer looks at her watch and then at the house. She says politely but assertively to the realtor, "Forget it. We have a lot of houses to see today and I can't waste my time on a house that doesn't have what I need." The house may have been exquisite if the buyer had only stepped inside. However, the buyer has neither the time nor the resources to search for value. Many other houses are available in the marketplace, and these houses make it easier for the buyer to immediately spot what she wants. This builder loses an opportunity because he forgot that selling begins during the first interaction.

The same discussion goes on within many companies searching for employees. The first interaction is key. The employer doesn't have the patience nor the resources to search through each candidate's cover letter hoping to uncover value. The candidate's value must be easy to spot, quickly and concisely.

In order to make your value easy for the employer to spot, each element in your career preparation must be planned. In your cover letter, you must introduce yourself to the employer in 20 seconds or less, and you must immediately sell your abilities to an employer. Thus, a cover letter is yet another narrative that ignites the reader's interest.

Since you have now concluded the writing of your award winning *The College Student's Step-By-Step Guide To Landing A Job* resumé, it's time to begin your next narrative, writing an effective cover letter. A cover letter is closely related to a resumé, in that both documents persuasively communicate you. And like a resumé, a cover letter possesses many of the same goals, including:

Readable: The cover letter's layout is graphically appealing and easy to read. The reader's attention gravitates to the important information.

Concise: All words are intentional and none are wasted. You minimize words whenever possible, use active verbs and never use personal pronouns.

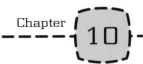
Crystal-Clear: The reader easily understands the cover letter, its language and images. The cover letter outlines your background and value.

Ignites Interest: The cover letter is interesting and describes experiences rather than tells about responsibilities. It creates a compelling story of value.

Transmits: The cover letter clearly communicates that you possess targeted skills.

Now that you have an idea of the cover letter's objective, it's time to understand the goal for writing each specific cover letter. Ideally, you must decide what each cover letter should state to the employer.

But where do you find the information? You'll find it from one of the easiest sources, the job description for a position you desire. The job description provides you with the needs of an employer. In its most basic form, a job description is the employer communicating to you. He or she is asking, "Do you have these skills and experiences? If you do, please write me and tell me about them. We may be able to talk in the near future."

Thus, it only makes sense to begin to dissect a job description into key skills and experiences. By doing this breakdown, you'll have a guide of what needs be written in the cover letter.

But don't forget:
Occasionally position descriptions contain a range of skill sets. You will want to prioritize your findings. After you dissect the description, highlight the skills which you have identified through your research as the most important to an employer. Then, do another prioritization. Place a check mark by the skills and experiences that are sought by the employer which you possess. These skills and experiences are the ones you will select to highlight in your cover letter.

APPRENTICESHIP

Making A Checklist

In *The College Student's Step-By-Step Guide To Landing A Job* apprenticeship, you will review two hypothetical job descriptions. To the right side of the job description, you will notice our checklist. To assist you in becoming as efficient as possible, it only makes sense to show you how to break down a job description into its key parts. Remember, the checklist is a great resource to provide you with direction on the key elements you should include in your cover letter.

The Jackson Group specializes in fields of industrial manufacturing. Specifically, The Jackson Group provides customers with in-depth consulting for businesses involved in traditional, capital intensive industries.

As our firm has grown substantially, the Jackson Group has opened an **entry-level civil engineering position.** For this position, you will work on-site with one of our major customers. You will manage a preventative maintenance program and will lead your team to ensure the highest level of customer service.

Upon continued growth, your duties may be enriched and expanded.

In the future, you may be responsible for basic human resource functions, and expanded management duties, such as providing scheduling and direction, providing performance reviews and discipline and resolving major consumer problems.

The candidate should possess the following skill sets:
1) A degree in civil engineering or related degree
2) Strong technical writing skills
3) Experience in leading a team(s)
4) Ability to analyze and present data.
5) A willing attitude to travel/work in the field for intermittent periods
6) A thorough understanding of Microsoft Word and Excel and AutoCAD software

Interested candidates should send a cover letter and resumé to:
The Jackson Group
1313 10th Avenue
Job, SD 00001.

Checklist

Before you begin writing your cover letter and preparing your resumé, develop a checklist of the key skills the employer seeks.

In this example, you will need to show the employer you possess the majority of the following skills.
• Customer service skills

• A degree in engineering

• Writing skills

• Leadership skills

• Data analysis skills

• A willingness to travel

• Proficiency with Microsoft Excel and Word and computer aided drafting software

Knowing the position's responsibilities may be expanded, you may want to proactively communicate:
• Skills in scheduling and prioritizing

• Teamwork skills

• Experience leading teams

• Conflict resolution skills

94

At *The College Student's Step-By-Step Guide To Landing A Job* **Career Services Center**, we're expanding our career services and recruitment division.

As an **entry level recruiter**, you will be responsible for a number of job activities, including the coordination and scheduling of phone interviews with candidates; updating job candidate profiles and providing strong customer service to candidates and our corporate clients.

In order to be considered for the position, you must possess a bachelor's degree. Additionally, you should have a minimum of six months experience in sales, human resources or recruiting. You should have experience in the Microsoft applications, including Outlook and Word; possess a typing speed of 35 words per minute. Because you will be dealing with internal and external clients, your written and verbal communication skills must be strong and your teamwork skills must be exceptional; your flexibility and willingness to prioritize must have been exhibited previously.

Checklist

In this example, the organization seeks an entry level recruiter. Unlike the previous example, this position description does not highlight key skills using bullet points.

You will need to sift through the position description to determine the major skills and experiences the employer wants.

- Scheduling skills

- Persistence to follow-up

- Customer service

- A bachelors degree

- Sales, human resource or recruiting experience (perhaps through an internship, jobs, class practicums)

- Technology skills with Microsoft applications

- Verbal and written communication skills

- Prioritization skills

-- APPRENTICESHIP --

The Nuts & Bolts Of A Cover Letter

Now that you know the key skills and experiences the employer is seeking, it's time to take the next step of award winning writers, developing an outline. Great authors often talk about an outline they prepare before they work. The outline serves as a guide for the direction of the writing. The outline also ensures all of the characters, plots and subplots are cohesive.

As you write *The College Student's Step-By-Step Guide To Landing A Job* award winning cover letter, you may also want to incorporate an outline. Your outline may include:

Section One:
- Explain why you are writing. Express your interest and specify the position
- Express how you learned about the position.
- Express your desire for the position.

Section Two:
- Express the values/skills/experiences you would bring to the position and how they align with the targeted skills for the position. Sell the experiences and benefits that are worthwhile to the employer.

Section Three:
- Close and provide a phone number and e-mail address.
- Be sure to spell all names and addresses correctly. Details are essential.
- Express everything with a positive tone. This is not the time and place to be humble or self-deprecating.

Ms. Dana Internship
Corporate Staffing Services
Jackson Corporation
124 Locks Street
Jackson, MO 00001

Dear Ms. Internship:

I am submitting my resumé in response to the Electrical Engineering position posted on your website.

I will receive an engineering degree from the University of Landing A Job in May 2005. As you will note, I rank in the top 20% of engineering majors and possess two internship experiences.

As my resumé details, my background combines academic and professional experience in electrical engineering and a demonstrated record of initiative and results.

My achievements include:

* **Recognized record of initiative and motivation:** Received an exceeds on two internship performance evaluations.

* **Electrical engineering experience professionally and academically:** Received a grade of A in all 18 credit hours of engineering and received 2000 hours of actual on-site engineering experience during two internships.

* **Proficiency in two major programming languages:** Marketplace experience and projects involving two programming languages, C++ and HTML.

I hope to have the opportunity to speak with you about the position. My goal is to contact you during the week of February 12, 2007. If I may provide you with any other information, please feel free to contact me at 133.000.0000 or through e-mail at jon.land@collegestudent.com.

Thank you for your time and consideration.

Sincerely,

Jon Land

Section One:
In the first paragraph, you will introduce yourself to the employer and identify the targeted position.

Section Two:
In the second section, you will communicate the value that you will add to the organization. If you have a job description via a classified or online ad, you should highlight the experiences and skills which address the job listing. If you do not have a job description, use the information that you collected through your industry research.

One of the most effective ways to address the job description is by using bullet points. The bullet points provide a cue to the reader and emphasize the importance of the section. Your bullet points come from the R and T section of the DART Principle in the *The College Student's Step-by-Step Guide to Landing A Job:* Career Toolkit.

Section Three:
The final section closes the cover letter. The section is comprised of your contact information. Additionally, the section thanks the employer and assertively asks for an interview.

APPRENTICESHIP

But where do you find this information, especially for the second section regarding your skills and experiences? The first source is *The College Student's Step-By-Step Guide To Landing A Job: Career Toolkit.* As you'll remember, it is full of your skills, abilities, and experiences. And you've developed stories about specific experiences that will be easy to modify for your cover letter. Additionally, you developed a key skills section for use in your resumé. If the skills align to the job description, you will also integrate them into the second section of the cover letter. For instance, let's take a look at an example of our hypothetical student's DART story.

Example of my initiative and leadership

Description: *For past three years 2001 - 2004, Foothills Softball Association could not afford new uniforms for children 8-10. Annual fundraising efforts had been stalled.*

Action: *As newly installed treasurer, I had two goals. Ensure spending is controlled and initiate fundraising efforts. Enlisted 12 volunteers, 4 local businesses and all participants. Ensured collaboration of entire committee. Initiated new fundraising effort.*

Results: *Fund-raiser netted $5,000 in funds and allowed uniform purchases. Largest fund-raiser in history of association. Received letter of commendation from association president.*

Takeaway: *I believe a strong key to leadership is initiative as well as collaboration. This example displays my type of leadership.*

The **Action and Results** sections provide you with key skills and experiences for the second section of your cover letter.

For instance, this student may choose to write:

My key skills include:
Leadership: *As the treasurer of a local community organization, I developed and led the largest fund raiser in the history of the organization.*

The **Key Skills** section of your resumé also provides you with a range of skills and experiences you can use in your cover letter.

For instance, our hypothetical student may write:

My key skills include:

Leadership: *As the treasurer of a local community organization, I developed and led the largest fund raiser in the history of the organization.*

Proven sales experience:
I possess two years of consumer retail sales and I was recognized by the organization with the highest sales performance award.

KEY SKILLS
_____

Possess academic and actual experience in public relations: 18 undergraduate hours in public relations and over 1000 internship hours with University Sports Information Director's Office.

Proven sales experience: Two years direct-to-consumer sales at national retail outlet. Received highest sales performance award given by retailer.

Ability to multi-task and meet deadlines and priorities: Worked over 20 hours per week to solely finance education. Able to maintain A-average with full academic course load and responsibilities for employment and internship.

Demonstrated leadership and teamwork: Led two-person student team for three years and community volunteer organization for one year. Maintained strong teams and received strong results.

Now it's your turn to start writing your cover letter. Remember, start by dissecting each position description so that you talk directly to the employer. Then make an outline of the three key sections. Finally, populate your outline and begin writing an award winning cover letter.

As a final apprenticeship, we've included another cover letter.

Ms. Dana Internship
Corporate Staffing Services
Jackson Corporation
124 Locks Street
Jackson, MO 00001

Dear Ms. Internship:

I am very interested in the Jackson Corporation's journalism internship opportunities. As a University of Success student, I view the position as an excellent opportunity to assist the Jackson Corporation by applying my diverse journalism experience and educational background.

As my resumé details, my background combines experience in the journalism field with a demonstrated record of results. My achievements include:

- Public Relations Experience: Writing the public relations plan for a $50 million dollar financial institution and its 4 branches
- Experienced in direct marketing: Teaming with other advertising practicum members to develop persuasive direct mail copy for the state's tourism bureau. Over 12 mailings were developed and the largest mailing garnered a return rate of 20%
- Development of advertising: Cooperatively working with an advertising agency to coordinate advertising executions
- Demonstrated leadership: Leading a multi-department team for the preparation and introduction of a relational marketing database system

Through these experiences, I truly believe that I will be able to assist the Jackson Corporation in accomplishing its objectives as I continue to actively learn about the publishing industry.

I hope to have the opportunity to speak with you about this position. If you need any other information, please feel free to contact me at (319)333-3333 or through e-mail at joan-lails@usuccess.edu.

Thank you for your time and consideration.

Sincerely,
Joan Lails

APPRENTICESHIP

APPRENTICESHIP

Cover Letter Writing Tips

DO

Invest the extra time to address your cover letter to a specific person.

Consider limiting your cover letter to one page.

Use strong language and statements in your cover letter. Use your work in *The College Student's Step-By-Step Guide To Landing A Job: Career Toolkit's* DART Principle section.

Review the language you use in your cover letter. Use concise, active verbs and minimize non-value-added words.

Use a similar aesthetic style on your cover letter and resumé. Print your cover letter on a bright, white paper stock. This makes it easier for an employer to scan and/or copy your cover letter and distribute it to others in the organization.

DON'T

Forget your cover letter and resumé are your introduction to an employer. Work diligently on your cover letter and ensure it addresses the key skills the employer seeks.

Use normal copy paper stock. Leverage even the smallest details, such as a quality paper stock, to make a strong impression with the employer.

Print your cover letter on a colored paper stock. The color makes copying difficult.

Take any chances on how the employer will receive your cover letter. Place your resumé and cover letter in a 9 inch by 12 inch envelope.

Forget to sign your cover letter.

Chapter Summary

Writing An Award Winning Cover Letter

Your cover letter is your 20-second introduction to an employer.
The document synthesizes your abilities to the employer and hopefully ignites her interest.

In order to successfully craft a compelling cover letter, you must understand the key skills and experiences an employer seeks.

By using the position description and your research on the industry, develop a checklist of key skills for the position.

Next, prioritize the skill sets. As you write your cover letter, you will want to display you possess a minimum of five of the skill sets.

Once you identify the skill sets, begin to write the cover letter. A persuasive cover letter contains three key sections:

- **In section one,** you introduce yourself to the employer and identify the position you for which you are applying.

- **In section two,** you communicate the value you will add to the organization. In this section, you will show how your experiences and skills match the employer's needs. This section is ideal for using the R (results) and T (takeaway) from *The College Student's Step-By-Step Guide To Landing A Job:* Career Toolkit as well as the Key Skills section on your resumé.

- **In section three,** you will close the letter. Be sure to thank the interviewer and assertively ask for an interview.

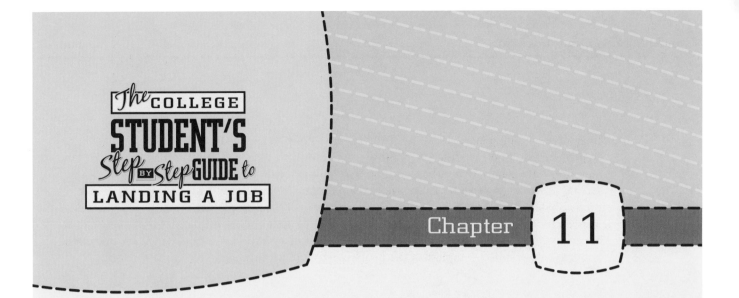

Chapter 11

The Thank You Note

Details matter. Use your
thank you note to give yourself
a strategic advantage over
your competition.

Imagine attending a local art fair with the intention of purchasing an oil painting for your apartment. You find two different paintings with similar styles, size, subject matter and price tags. You fully believe that either painting will look fantastic in your home. However, the second artist offers a frame to accentuate the painting's texture, subtle tones and hues. The frame obviously is of little value in and of itself; however, because it was hand selected by the artist herself, it accentuates the work perfectly, highlighting the same qualities that caught your eye in the first place. Which painting do you purchase? Clearly the advantage goes to the artist going the extra mile to emphasize the benefits that initially attracted you to the artwork.

Make the extra effort.
Use personalized thank you notes to your advantage.

In the same manner as a free frame for a painting, a finishing touch in the interview process can differentiate you from your competition. As a job candidate, you are in a marketplace, just like an artist at a local art fair. Employers have a number of options to choose from. What will make them choose you?

Remember, the selection process does not stop with the interview. Even if you experienced a great interview, were well prepared and believe you performed exceptionally well, it's time to capitalize on it. You must strategically plan your next move.

Challenge yourself to think differently. Each opportunity to communicate with the prospective employer is extremely important. Thus, use a thank you note as another tool which helps you to reinforce your value to their organization.

The personalized thank you note can differentiate you from other candidates.

Your Toolkit
Remember, be meaningful and be different. Differentiate yourself from the competition and do not just send an e-mailed note.

Instead, try a different approach. Within 12 hours after the interview, send a concise e-mail note to each of your interviewer(s). In the e-mail note, relay your appreciation for their time and express you are excited about the job and want it.

Then, the real work begins. Within 24 hours, mail a typed, formal thank you note to all of your interviewers. A thank you note contains a number of key components, which are shown on the following apprenticeship.

A Quick Note: Be Timely.
Send Your Thank You Note Within 24 Hours. Be efficient. Buy a package of thank you notes or begin typing your note immediately after you return home. Because some hiring decisions are made within a day if not hours after an interview, it may be to your advantage to send a brief but professional thank you note by e-mail as soon as possible after your interview. However, this does not make you exempt from sending a formal thank you note via mail.

The Key Components In Your Thank You Note

1) Express gratitude for the opportunity. Be specific about the areas of appreciation.

2) Reinforce your interest and enthusiasm for the position and express you want the position.

3) Consider using the typed thank you note as a way to address a question you may not have answered fully during the interview.

4) Succinctly reinforce why you fit with the company.

5) Express everything with a positive tone.

6) Send the note the day after the interview.

7) Make it short and sweet. Simplicity is a form of discipline. If your letter conveys the key objectives in a moderate number of words, it shows you truly thought about what you wanted to state and worked diligently on the thank you note.

8) To ensure you spell everyone's name correctly, politely ask for a business card after your interview.

-- APPRENTICESHIP --

December 31, 2005

Mr. John P. Success
Managing Partner
Stone-Throw Engineering
831 Canary Avenue
Johnson, NY 00001

Dear Mr. Success:

I wanted to thank you for your time and the opportunity to discuss with you the Engineering Consultant position. I appreciated all of your thoughts regarding the company's corporate culture as well as the key skill sets Stone-Throw Engineering targets for its incoming employees.

As we discussed, I am confident I have the targeted skill sets including a demonstrated record of initiative and results as well as the application of the required engineering skills.

I am extremely excited about the position and look forward to speaking with you next week. If I can provide you with more information, please contact me and I will send it to you.

Thanks again.

Sincerely,

Joan Johnson

APPRENTICESHIP

Mr. Alan Employer
Ecto Shoe Brand
Jordan, WI 00001

Dear Mr. Employer:

Thank you for the opportunity to meet on December 11. I truly appreciated our discussion regarding the Ecto Shoe Brand.

As I mentioned in our conversation, the goal of my career search is to find an optimal level of organizational fit. Through our discussion of Ecto Shoe Brand's corporate philosophy, the value it places on its people, and the firm's cooperative spirit, I became even more enthusiastic about the organization.

I truly am excited about the career opportunities and look forward to the potential of joining the team.

Thank you for the time. I sincerely appreciated it.

Sincerely,

Jack Success
39082 Plaza Drive.
Jackson, SC 00001

Writing Effective Thank You Notes

DO

Proactively prepare for writing thank you notes. Ask each interviewer for his/her respective business card and confirm the correct spelling of each individual with your contact person.

After each interview, write a small reminder to yourself about the discussion in your padfolio. You will use this information in your thank you note.

Immediately (within 12 hours) follow-up on an interview with a concise, brief professional e-mail thank you.

Immediately mail a typed thank you note.

Check and recheck each thank you note before you send it. Make sure to spell each individual's name correctly and use correct grammar.

Use the typed thank you note as a way to address a question you may not have answered fully during the interview.

Buy a gaggle of stamps ahead of time.

Make sure the e-mail thank you and the typed thank you note information are different.

DON'T

Guess at the spelling of an interviewer's name.

Just e-mail a thank you note to each interviewer. Remember, your goal is to make a strong impression with each individual. A fifty-cent thank you note may be worth a $30,000 plus job.

Copy a thank you note from the campus placement office or website. Imagine the employer's shock when he/she gets multiple thank you letters that are all the same. Differentiate yourself through a well thought out personalized note.

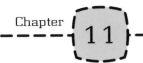

Chapter Summary

The Thank You Note

Use thank you notes strategically.
While many candidates send thank you notes because they feel it is customary, a thank you note can serve as a strategic method to reinforce your value to an employer.

To aid in writing a thank you note, proactively plan a few action steps during the interview.
Ask for a business card from each interviewer.

Ensure you have a document (such as an itinerary) which correctly spells each interviewer's full name before your interview concludes.

After each interview, jot down a few notes regarding your discussion. You will cite this information in your thank you notes.

Most thank you notes have three components:
1) An expression of gratitude for the opportunity and the time.

2) A reinforcement of your interest in the position and the company and/or an opportunity to answer a difficult question which you may not have answered satisfactorily.

3) A direct expression of your interest in the position.

Remember, thank you notes are time-sensitive.
Send a brief e-mail thank you note within 12 hours after your interview. Then, mail a full, typed thank you note to the interviewer within 24 hours.

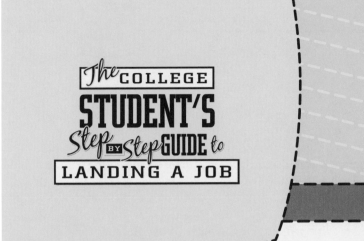

Chapter 12

Writing And Following A Script: The Act Of Interviewing

The beginning and the ending of our conversations are too important to leave to chance.

Have you ever seen a script for a movie or a play? Did you notice how every element is spelled out? Dialogue is written, expressions are described and movements are choreographed. Why? Because in a limited amount of time, the characters must be developed, a plot must be communicated and the movie must be intriguing for the viewer. These goals cannot occur without specifying each and every detail. Very little can be left to chance or interpretation.

Employers script interviews just like writers script movies. Why? Because the employer faces the same type of time constraint as a script writer. The interviewer must proactively plan the interview to ensure being able to determine in a short amount of time if the candidate meets all of the needed qualifications.

First and last impressions are
too important to leave to chance

A job interview closely resembles theater.
Thus, you, the college student, must transform yourself beyond someone simply interviewing for a position. You must emulate an actor, pure and simple.

The employer has a script of questions which he or she must ask each and every candidate. Your goal is to create interest in your character. You must display the passion of your character and encourage the audience (the interviewer) to want more.

So with this knowledge, you know what lies ahead. It's time to emulate the process of writing a script and acting the scenes. Your goal is to win the Academy Awards of screen writing and acting in your own movie called, My Interview. Let's begin by rolling out the red carpet and by learning about introductions.

> You create a strong impression at the beginning and end of each interview.

Imagine opening night of a new musical on Broadway. Picture the lights, glamour, excitement, and yes, critics. Is there any doubt that this first night will make or break the entire run of the show? If the lead actor or actress is having an off night, it will dramatically affect the reviews in the paper the next day, which in turn will determine whether or not the general public will be willing to wait in line for hours and pay an exorbitant price for tickets to future shows. Entire productions have been cancelled based on public response from opening night.

Your opening night is your first few moments in the interview.
Can you recollect a time when you first met someone? How quickly did you create an impression of the person? Was it within the first minute? Or did you create a perception of the person in under 30 seconds? As you learned in Writing an Award Winning Cover Letter, the value of first impressions is significant in any endeavor and that is especially true when interviewing.

To master the craft of interviewing, you must understand the importance of a great beginning (as well as a great ending). Unfortunately, the beginning and the ending of the interview are often the most overlooked and unrehearsed portions of the interview. In this section you will learn about constructing a powerful introduction. Then you will learn about the proper method to close an interview. No matter what type of interview you undergo, both exercises are extremely applicable.

Your Introduction

At the start of an interview, you have an ideal opportunity to create a perception of your skills and your value. In fact, many interviewers discreetly ask you to detail your value at the beginning of the interview by asking the seemingly innocuous question, "Why don't you tell me a little about yourself?"

You can reasonably translate the question to, "What about you would make you valuable to my organization?" The interviewer is interested in you, but the emphasis is on your value. Don't be mislead into thinking this question is just small talk to break the ice and make you feel comfortable.

Your Tools

The key here lies in strategically using the introduction to reinforce your value to the employer. To create this perception of value, keep the following strategies in your mind and script out your introductory statement.

Introductions:
Concentrate on the three major reasons that make you valuable to the interviewer.

You will summarize this information in your introduction.

Approach this introduction as the first opportunity to sell yourself to the employer.

1) Take the time to develop your introductory statement and make sure you rehearse it.

2) Use a chronological overview. Outline your various experiences and major accomplishments in order. As you relay your introduction, highlight any accomplishments, skills and experiences which directly relate to the position for which you are applying.

3) Your statement should be concise and to the point. The total introduction should not exceed one minute. Don't delve into the major details. Instead, concentrate on the three major reasons that make you valuable to the organization.

Now that you have an idea of the key strategies to use in an introduction script, it's time to review a few samples of them. Four examples are attached. After you have read each example and the key objectives for each introduction, it's your turn to apply your learning. *Turn to The College Student's Step-By-Step Guide To Landing A Job: Career Toolkit.* The next exercise is the BLUEPRINT FOR SUCCESS: INTRODUCTIONS AND CLOSINGS. Use the tools in this chapter to write an introductory statement script.

APPRENTICESHIP

One of the quickest methods to prepare an introduction is by reviewing a few examples. As you read the following statements, note their precision and their ability to demonstrate the student's value to the employer. Each of the forthcoming statements follows the outline provided on the previous page.

An introductory statement for an entry-level marketing communication position.

My name is Jon Success. I've been extremely fortunate due to my experiences. I will have a degree in business and psychology in May 2005 at the University of Stone. I believe the combination provides an ideal blend of the science of marketing with the art of understanding people. But what I'm most appreciative about is my practical experience. Over the past three years, I've held three internships. One with a marketing research firm, one with an advertising agency and one at the university's public relations department. During this time, my projects included writing copy for advertising and press releases, conducting quantitative analysis and presenting analysis to management. I've truly enjoyed the marketing communication area, and I think my passion has been reflected in my past performance evaluations at the internships; I received exceeded expectation ratings at all three internships. And now I'm truly excited about the opportunity with your firm and learning more about it today.

An introductory statement for an entry-level engineering position.

Hi, my name is Jill Success. I am extremely interested in engineering. In the spring, I will receive a degree in chemical engineering at Stone University. Over the past four years, I have attempted to expose myself to as much of the engineering discipline as possible. I have had two practicums and two internships in the petroleum industry. Through this experience, I learned a strong engineer needs to not only understand the science of engineering, she must also be able to effectively communicate. Thus, I served as an active member in the university's Toastmaster club and a reporter for the university newspaper. I am very interested in the position and I am looking forward to our conversation today to learn more about the opportunity and your firm.

An introductory statement for an entry-level sales position.

It's a pleasure meeting with you Mr. Mployee. I wanted to thank you for taking this time to meet with me because I understand how busy you must be. First of all, let me tell you that I've been very fortunate in gaining a great deal of experience in sales. In my marketing courses, I've taken 18 credit hours, 12 of which have been regarding sales, personal selling and sales promotions. This background has really assisted me to understand the selling process and the key components of persuasion, which ultimately has helped me be more successful in my job. I've applied many of the key principles of buying behavior, including gaining attention and driving conviction in my position at Big John's Electronic Super Store. In fact, I've recently been the top salesperson for two of the past 14 months at the store. Additionally, because I've worked approximately 20 hours a week and also maintained a full class load, I've learned key prioritization skills. In fact, I believe my ability to manage my time and prioritize key projects will be truly useful in this position. I am truly interested in learning more about this opportunity.

An introductory statement for an entry-level management position.

It's a pleasure meeting with you Mr. Mployee. Thank you for your time and opportunity. I am truly excited about our conversation. First of all, I have an strong sense of persistence and initiative. I currently work 30 hours a week managing a local clothing store and still maintain a 3.2 grade point average. In fact, in my management and accounting classes, my grade point average exceeds a 3.5. Due to my academic and work schedule, I've learned that it's necessary to possess strong time management skills and a clear focus. Additionally, I've also learned the key to clear communication. As a student working in many group projects and as a manager with over five employees, I know the value of communicating precisely, often and consistently. I believe that's why our retail outlet is consistently rated high during mystery shopper visits. I'm looking forward to learning more about your organization and the skills it prizes.

Effective Introductory Statements

The following outline serves as a quick guide to create an introductory statement.

Time limit: 60 seconds or less

Part 1: State who you are.

Part 2: Provide a concise overview of your experience and accomplishments. Your major theme should be, "Briefly describe what makes you valuable and qualified for this position."

Think of the three key points you want to make to the interviewer. Make sure to communicate the major areas that highlight what is important to the employer. These major areas should be specific. Avoid generic statements, such as, "I have a great deal of initiative and like people."

Instead, summarize key experiences that have helped you develop valuable skills. To structure this information, use this fill-in-the-blank formula to describe three major reasons why the interviewer should hire you.

"Because of this experience, I have this skill to offer you."

"Because of this training, I have this experience or skill to offer you."

"Because of this accomplishment, I can do this."

You may also want to reference *The College Student's Step-By-Step Guide To Landing A Job* resumé. The Key Skills section provides a nice concise summary of your key skills.

Part 3: Express how enthusiastic you are about the organization and the interview process. This is the key element. You must explicitly tell the interviewer you want the job.

-- APPRENTICESHIP --

APPRENTICESHIP

The Closing Statement

Have you ever watched a movie and been enthralled all of the way through only to be disappointed in the direction the plot turned at the end? What comes to your mind when a friend asks how you liked the movie? Is your reaction to detail the middle of the story or to verbalize your discontent with the ending?

The same importance should be placed at the end of a conversation. At the end of an interview, you have one final opportunity to reinforce your skills, value and interest to the employer–your closing statement.

An experienced interviewer will often elicit a closing statement by asking a question like, "Are there any other questions or anything else you'd like to discuss before this session ends?" This is your opportunity to reaffirm your value. Remember, an interviewer wants you to "want" the job. An interviewer's job is to recruit and retain employees. Do not be apprehensive about telling the interview that you want the job.

Your Tools

This is the last impression you will leave with the interviewer, so a well prepared and rehearsed closing statement is imperative. Once again, you must be concise. You should target 30-90 seconds for your statement.

The key components for an effective closing are as follows:
1) Reinforce your interest in the company and the industry.
2) Reinforce your skills and value. Remember to be as specific as possible.
3) Provide the interviewer with one more opportunity to collect additional information.
4) Reinforce that you **WANT** the position. Be direct in expressing your interest in the position.

The following examples are intended to provide direction in creating your own closing statement. As you'll note, each of the statements follow the discussed outline. After you have read the example, begin work on an introductory and closing statement on *The College Student's Step-By-Step Guide To Landing A Job: Career Toolkit*.

Example 1: Thank you for the opportunity. From our discussion, I am extremely excited about the position. The culture appears to be a nice fit and I appreciate the ongoing development opportunities. I also believe I have the skills to add to your organization. I believe my exposure to the different areas of marketing communication along with my history of results can assist your organization. And I am very willing to develop my skill set even more. I am very interested in this position and want this opportunity. Before we end today, are there any questions which I may not have fully answered? Also, would you be willing to discuss the next steps in the process and if there is any more information I can provide you? I want to tell you in no uncertain terms, I want this position.

Example 2: Thank you for the opportunity. I really enjoyed our conversation and I appreciate all of the information you provided regarding the key skill sets the company is looking for and the company's culture and people. From our discussion, I believe I possess many of the skills you alluded to, including strong quantitative skills and effective communication skills. As we discussed, I have had three internships within the industry and have exceeded expectations in all three internships. My goal is to bring this type of work ethic to your organization. I am very interested in this opportunity. Are there any questions that I should answer more fully? Also, what do you see as the next steps in the process?

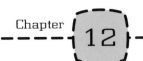

Chapter Summary

Interview Introductions and Closings

First and last impressions are extremely important.
However, many college candidates fail to maximize these opportunities.

To make your interview as effective as possible, plan your introduction and closing statements. Write a sample introduction and closing in *The College Student's Step-By-Step Guide To Landing A Job: Career Toolkit.*

Introductory Statements:
The key to "telling a little bit about yourself" lies in three key steps:
1) State who you are.

2) Provide a concise overview of your experience and accomplishments.

3) Express your enthusiasm about the organization and the interview process.

Closing Statements:
A closing statement provides you with a final opportunity to reinforce your value to an interviewer.

The key for a closing statement includes:
1) Reinforce your interest in the company and the industry.

2) Reinforce your skills and your value.

3) Provide the interviewer with one more opportunity to collect additional information.

4) Ask for the position.

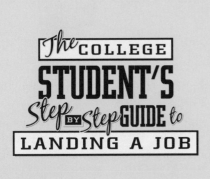

Chapter 13

Preparing A Script
For An Interview

Now that you understand the value you can contribute to an organization, it's time to learn the method to communicate your value.

Preparing for an interview is like acting in a movie

In the previous chapter, you began to write the introduction and closing of a script. Now, it's time to write the body. Like a movie script, we're going to develop a plot as well as the character. Luckily, you are the main character, so you'll be able to draw upon the incredible knowledge you've developed about yourself over the last couple of decades.

As you have already learned, a number of interviewers read a script of questions which are predetermined before the interview even begins. The questions search for specific key skills and areas of value. Your key is knowing which questions have the greatest probability to be asked and being able to answer them in a compelling, substantial and persuasive manner. By doing your homework in the previous Difference Between Talent and Genius section of *The College Student's Step-By-Step Guide To Landing A Job*, you are tilting the odds in your favor for being able to do just that.

Successful interviewing involves writing a script of your answers.

One type of interview that is commonly used is behavioral-based selection. Behavioral-based selection relies on the axiom, "Your past behavior serves as an indication of your future behavior."

For example, let's imagine you apply for an entry-level accounting position. Your previous experience includes a work-study position with the university's finance department. During your tenure, you found two ways to save the university $3,000 versus the previous year. To a prospective employer this example shows you previously displayed a key ability, the ability to control spending. Behavioral-based selection suggests that since you are able to control spending today, you have a greater potential to exhibit this key skill set in the future.

Behavioral-based selection is not a perfect method and you may find some debate regarding the technique's effectiveness. However, you will find a significant number of employers using this interview method. So regardless of your personal feelings about this interview method, it is in your best interest to expect this type of encounter and be prepared for it.

Strategically, a behavioral-based selection process benefits the candidate. The technique challenges job candidates to: 1) understand their value and, 2) communicate their value in an persuasive and specific manner. Thus, think of a behavioral-based interview process as an ideal method to aid in your preparation for becoming the expert on you.

Background

Again, the behavioral-based interview process is straight forward. The interviewer believes certain key skills and experiences will create value to their organization; and that if a candidate has exhibited these skills in the past he or she has the potential to exhibit them in the future. The objective for the employer is to find candidates who possess these skill sets. Therefore, the interviewer is charged with uncovering whether you have exhibited the desired skills in the past.

To do so, the interviewer asks a litany of questions designed to uncover your past performance with these skill sets. The interviewer searches for the targeted key skill sets by looking for examples on a resumé and asking specific questions of the candidate. For instance, an interviewer may need to confirm you possess key leadership skills and say, "Tell me about a time when you were asked to lead a group."

Cracking The Code

In order to be successful, you must identify the skill or behavior the interviewer is seeking. After listening to a question, you may think to yourself, "The interviewer is looking for leadership."

Once identified, you must construct an example describing a situation in which you demonstrated your skills in question. For instance:

"In my senior year, I was elected president of the university's music society. For the previous 10 years, the society was unable to recruit more than three new members per year. Seeing the need to focus on recruitment, I organized a recruiting/membership committee of 10 society and faculty members, developed a recruiting plan and ultimately recruited over 20 individuals, the most recruited in one year. Now the music society has the most members in the Fine Arts Department; the society is extremely strong and has a long-term recruiting plan. I think this shows leadership is the ability to understand the major issues, focus on the most important needs and effectively implement programs that generate meaningful results."

Did you notice the precision of the answer? Sounds great doesn't it? It's the DART Principle you worked on earlier.

Notice the inclusion of all 4 DART Principle elements: Description (the society was unable to effectively recruit new members), Action (I organized a recruiting committee, developed a recruiting plan), Result (the committee recruited the most members in one year, the society is strong and has a long-term plan), and Take-away (I demonstrated leadership by understanding the issue, focusing on needs and implementing programs that generated meaningful results).

Luckily, you have already developed a number of examples to include in your interviewing script. And now because of this work, you have a number of narratives prepared for the interview situation.

Your Tools

But wait, you haven't formalized your script yet. The official *The College Student's Step-By-Step Guide To Landing A Job* Script For Interviewing involves understanding how the questions may be asked in an interview. After all, you need to be prepared. The following apprenticeship shows you the question format often used in behavioral interviews.

Then it's your turn to begin writing an award winning script. Begin by reviewing each skill set that you found when you conducted your research. Next consider a potential behavioral-based question for the most sought after skills in your industry by mirroring the questions in the corresponding apprenticeship. Finally, make sure you have an appropriate narrative developed to exhibit each targeted skill set.

As you prepare for a behavioral interview, develop an impressive script for your interview. Make sure each of your DART narratives possesses the following key elements.

1) Always use I: Show your contribution. Employers are interviewing you for the job, not your team.

2) Always use past tense verbs. Structure your narrative to show employers you already have exhibited the skill.

3) Focus on being concise. The simpler and more concise the story, the more persuasive.

4) Focus on key information. The interviewer's time is also constrained. Make sure your narratives focus on the key skills the employer wants.

5) Use the employer's perspective. Make sure your narratives specifically discuss a certain skill set(s). A good story always has a point. Make sure your narratives tell a story about your skill set.

If an employer seeks the following skill (in bold) you may hear him or her ask you the following questions. The interviewer may ask these questions:

- **Leadership skills.**
  Have you ever led a group for a school project but were not the formal leader?

- **The ability to initiate.**
  Have you ever initiated a project in school, during an internship or in another organization and went beyond the call of duty?

- **Drive, persistence and tenacity.**
  Have you ever overcome another student's resistance to your point of view?

  Have you ever initially failed at a project but found a way to finish it?

  Tell me about your most difficult class and how you approached it.

- **Teamwork skills.**
  How do you ensure contributions by others, such as your fellow students on a class project?

  Can you describe a time you led a team in school or with another organization?

  Describe a time when you teamed with other students on a project.

- **Communication skills.**
  Have you ever given a well-received speech or presentation? What made it so successful?

  If you don't understand another person's point of view, describe the steps you would take to gain understanding?

- **Ability to handle challenge.**
  How do you handle disagreements with others?

- **Time management.**
  How do you manage to meet your daily goals?

  How do you ensure progress on your school projects or toward your degree?

- **Ability to motivate or captivate others.**
  What accomplishment are you most proud of? Why are you most proud of it?

  Describe a time you were involved in a university or other organizational group and needed to move the group toward a goal.

- **Problem solving.**
  Describe a time when you may not have had all the information you needed but were required to make a decision. How did you handle the situation?

- **Resolving conflicts.**
  Describe a time when you and a fellow student disagreed on a project. How did you handle the situation?

  Have you ever changed your style to become more effective?

  Tell me how you handle a difficult person.

  Have you experienced a difficult challenge during an internship or job situation?

APPRENTICESHIP

Chapter Summary

Preparing a Script for an Interview

Behavioral-based interviewing is fairly commonplace.
This interview method relies on the axiom, "Your past behavior serves as an indicator of your future behavior."

Leverage the research you've all ready completed in *The College Student's Step-By-Step Guide To Landing A Job*: Career Toolkit to answer this type of interview question.
Prepare by reviewing each skill set targeted by your industry.

Develop narratives to show that you have previously demonstrated each skill.

In response to behavioral-based questions:
Identify the skill the interviewer is seeking to uncover through their question.
Be sure to include all 4 elements of the DART Principle in your answer

D Description

A Action

R Result

T Takeaway

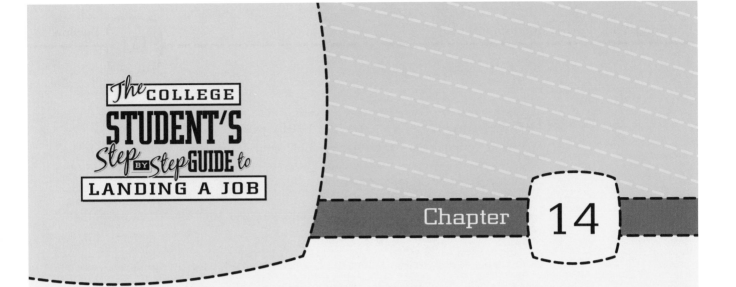

Chapter 14

Preparing For Other
Interview Techniques

Your best preparation for
an interview is to expose
yourself to a wide variety of
interviewing techniques.

Other Potential Scripts To Prepare

Similar to the movies or the theater, multiple genres exist in interviewing. While the behavior-based concept is the standard, there are other formats for which you must be prepared in order to ensure success.

One common interviewing technique attempts to gauge your understanding of the company, the industry or the position.

In this type of interview situation, the employer may ask basic questions such as:

"What do you know about our institution?"

"Why do you want to work at this fine institution?"

"What major observations can you make about our industry? How do you stay abreast of them?"

During the interview process, you may encounter other forms of interviewing techniques. You must be prepared.

In this interview situation, preparation is key. By conducting background research, you can provide a concise answer to each question. In fact, the previous "The Difference Between Talent and Pure Genius" chapter is devoted to assisting you in conducting this research. In this chapter, you researched key skill sets, became more familiar with the vocabulary specific to the industry and developed an effective reference tool to maintain an understanding of industry trends.

Additionally, you should begin writing scripts for each of these answers. Follow a similar objective as the one used in your opening and closing scripts. Make sure you express your interest, show your level of preparation by citing specific trends or research and concluding with a final statement that indicates you are interested in the industry and the company.

Theory Questions

In other instances, interviewers may ask an ambiguous question. The question may tempt you to respond with a generalization.

"What really motivates you personally and professionally?"

"How do you work if the pressure is on?"

"What would a few of your colleagues tell us about you? How about your boss?"

Don't fall prey to this technique and answer a general question with a general answer. If you choose this method, you have effectively lost an opportunity to display your value to the employer.

Instead, follow the DART Principle. **Use a specific example of a life experience to answer the question.**

For instance, theory questions should be answered in the same manner you would answer a behavioral-based question.

If you were asked, *"What would a few of your colleagues tell us about you? How about your boss?"* start your answer by stating the key takeaway, *"I believe my colleagues would say I have outstanding initiative. In fact, let me give you an example of why they would believe this....."* and then lead into the remaining elements of the DART, your description, your action, the result and key takeaway. Your goal is to provide a story about a life experience that demonstrates a key skill set.

> Don't respond to a general question with a general answer. Take the opportunity to give specifics on your value to the employer.

By using this technique, you are making the interviewer's job easier. You are not only communicating a valuable skill that you possess, but also providing a specific example that demonstrates your past history in reflecting that skill.

Critical Reasoning Questions

Interviewers also use case study and critical reasoning questions. The interviewer uses this technique to analyze your cognitive ability and reasoning skills. For example, an interviewer may ask you to estimate the total amount of coffee creamer consumed in the United States or the amount of chocolate consumed on average by each individual in the United States.

Does the interviewer really care about the answer?
Absolutely not! The interviewer is attempting to gauge your analysis and problem solving abilities.

Tools For Critical Reasoning Questions
The key to the case study question is to make basic assumptions and lead the interviewer through your pattern of reasoning.

> Critical reasoning questions should demonstrate your logic and analysis skills. The exact answer is not important. Your ability to communicate how you think and approach problems is the key.

Watch out:
Do not become a victim of a common pitfall by diving into the data. Instead make basic assumptions with easy-to-calculate numbers. In some interview situations, the interviewer will give you a pad and paper to show your thoughts and calculations. If they do not, make sure you always use easy-to-calculate numbers (like round multiples of 1000, 100, 10, etc.)

The critical reasoning type of question examines your ability to assess a problem and evaluate potential solutions. Analyzing a critical reasoning problem is straightforward, and entails three steps:

First, determine the objective. To do this, answer the question, "What is the key objective, goal, answer or challenge that needs to be addressed?"

Next, brainstorm three major options that could solve the challenge and explain them to the interviewer. You must answer the question, "What are the available alternatives?"

Third, evaluate the alternatives. Explain the advantages and disadvantages of each option. Finally, recommend an option. Explain your rationale for your choice. You must answer the question, "Why is this option advantageous versus the other options?"

If you are a business major, mass communication major or engineering major you may face a question intended to help the interviewer understand your ability to use major strategic models.

For instance a business major may be asked to utilize Porter's Five Forces or the Four P's of Marketing. A mass communication major may be asked to utilize the strategic process to develop a creative or media strategy. Therefore, it only makes sense to prepare for these opportunities. If you find through your research that you will face critical reasoning questions in your interview, consider developing a one to two page reference document which contains the major strategic models.

Again, you will want to review this script until you have memorized its key components.

APPRENTICESHIP

Example 1
If the question was to calculate the total amount of coffee consumption in the US, you may choose to approach it in this manner:

- 250 million people live in the U.S.A. The average household has approximately 2.5 people (whether it really does or not does not matter.) Strive to be reasonable but not precise. 250 is easily divisible by 2.5.

- That means approximately 100 million households. (The goal is to work with easy numbers for the calculation). If each household consumed approximately 4 canisters per year, this would equate to 400 million canisters.

- However, not every canister is uniform. Thus, let's say the average canister holds 16 ounces of coffee or 1 pound (remember, always try to find the easiest, relevant metric to calculate).

Then this would mean 400 million pounds of coffee.

Even When You Forget The Script, Don't Give Up

Even seasoned actors in the theater occasionally forget their lines or periodically have to face dreaded stage fright. Even with all of the hard work in preparing and rehearsing an award-winning script, the crippling condition still can leave them with a line just beyond their reach, a frustrating dilemma indeed.

Fortunately time will typically allow the actor to regroup and tackle the situation at hand with a compelling ad lib.

Similarly you may face a challenging interview question to which you have no immediate answer. Luckily, sufficient preparation does minimize this risk; however, that will do little to reassure you should the issue arise. The key here is to remain calm and not give the appearance of being frazzled. Be aware that it is perfectly fine to ask for a moment to compose an answer. One slant is to compliment the interviewer and state, "That's an interesting question, would you mind if I took a moment to contemplate my answer?"

While you cannot use the time-out for every question, it's perfectly acceptable to use it once during an interview.

Chapter Summary

Preparing for Other Interview Techniques

During your career preparation process, you will be exposed to a number of interview techniques.

Generalized Questions
Additionally, an interviewer may ask about your understanding of the company. For instance,
"What major observations can you make about our industry?"
The key: Utilize your previous research of the company and the organization.

Theory Questions
Many questions may seem basic or ambiguous, such as: *"What would a few of your colleagues tell us about you?"*

The key:
1) Do not respond with a generalization. Provide a solid example of how you exhibited the skill.

2) Reference the numerous narratives you developed in *The College Student's Step-By-Step Guide To Landing A Job:* Career Toolkit's DART Principle section.

Case Study Questions
You will on occasion face Case Study Questions. For instance, *"We gained dog food distribution at Wal-Mart. How much additional staffing will be required to service this account?"*

The key:
1) The "right" answer is not essential.

2) The interviewer is looking for your critical reasoning skills

3) Provide alternatives and explain how you came to your conclusion

You will undoubtedly face a question during your interviews that stumps you.
Take your time and remain calm.

Chapter 15

Body Language

If the majority of our message is communicated through our body language, why don't we practice it more often?

According to some research studies, approximately one-half or more of each message you convey is interpreted by the receiver via your nonverbal cues rather than the actual words you speak.

So what does this mean to you during your career preparation? It means body language is much more important than you may think. But how many times, do we even think about our body language? And have you ever heard a friend talk about working on his or her body language during an interview? "You know Jim, my answers were OK, but what really helped me land a job was posture and attentive body language."

— During an interview, you communicate much more than what you actually say. If a picture paints 1,000 words, your posture paints a million.

These subtle nuances are important. Body language and your other nonverbal cues communicate a message loud and clear. Think about how your favorite actors convey a mood and tone. Have you ever watched a foreign movie in the middle of the night? Even when the actor is speaking in a foreign language, you can understand the plot. Why? Because great actors know the majority of our messages are conveyed through our body language. They make it easy to distinguish their character's feelings, passion, confidence or despair. The distinction is clear and the message is communicated without a single word. In the same way, you set a tone in your interviews regardless of the actual words coming out of your mouth.

Clearly body language is important, so why don't more college candidates evaluate their own? Probably because it takes time and effort, and a fairly strong sense of self awareness. By proactively setting goals for your body language and practicing during mock interviews, you will enjoy an advantage over your competition.

What is good body language?

Great body language conveys a positive attitude as well as a keen sense of interest to the interviewer. Through your nonverbal actions you convey to the interviewer that you are interested in the position and that you are confident you possess the abilities that can create value for the employer. Poor body language conveys that you are tentative, unsure if you are qualified and potentially that you are not a right fit for the job.

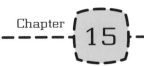

Your tool for strong body language starts with a positive mind and attitude.

So how do we begin? First we must start with a positive attitude. Have you ever seen a professional actor before his or her play started? They may be listening to music or sitting alone with their eyes closed or speaking their lines aloud. Are they thinking about their upcoming performance? Absolutely. In fact, even more than that, they are preparing for success. And *The College Student's Step-By-Step Guide To Landing A Job* believes you should consider the same approach. Prepare for success.

One hour before you go into an interview, you need to prepare for success. Take ten to twenty minutes to formally develop a positive attitude through a mental imagery exercise. First, imagine the interview. In your mind, imagine stepping into your first interviewer's office and the first thing you see the interviewer smile. The individual is extremely nice and excited to see you. Then see yourself smiling back at her. Now imagine your internal monologue saying inside of your head, "This is going to work out fantastic."

Then, imagine the interview. If you like, imagine each question the interviewer will ask and state aloud your answer. After each answer, imagine the interviewer smiling, nodding her head and genuinely giving you positive feedback.

As you move to the end of the interview, imagine you and your interviewer giving one another a strong handshake. You leave the office with a positive attitude, knowing you have the job.

Tips For Body Language

DO

Remember, no matter how you perceive the interviewer's disposition, ensure your body language is always positive. As any great actor, you must carry out the show. Sooner or later, you will win over your audience.

DON'T

Convey mixed messages: Your body language, your tone, your attitude and your spoken words must always be aligned. If they are not, you will send a mixed signal to the interviewer.

Does it sound a little corny? Maybe, if you are afraid what some imaginary person or imaginary society might say. Maybe if you choose to create fear in your mind rather than confidence. But it's time to rid yourself of such insecurities. It's time to prepare positively. It's time to Land A Job!

After this mental imagery exercise, it's time for a short positive internal talk. The goal of the internal talk is to become your biggest fan and give yourself a boost of confidence. For five to ten minutes, either write on a piece of paper or tell yourself internally, "I can do it. I am prepared. I'm going to do fantastic." You aren't just fooling yourself either. Considering the amount of time you have all ready put into your preparation through *The College Student's Step-By-Step Guide To Landing A Job* process. You are prepared and you can do it!

Think about the average candidate. Why does she get nervous? If the college student is prepared, why wouldn't she believe her preparation or performance will help her land the job? Often times, the candidate psyches herself out. She begins questioning her level of preparation or how she ranks against other candidates (whom she has never met and knows nothing about their level of preparation). And while she has all the tools to land the job, her own mind is her worst enemy. Your job is to become your biggest fan and not allow a negative attitude to get in your way.

Body Language Tips:
Remember, communication isn't just the string of words coming out of your mouth. Negative nonverbal signals can void all of the positive impact your preparation has built throughout the interview.

Negative Body Language
The following body positions and facial expressions convey merely moderate or negative interest:

1) Body angle: Leaning away from the interviewer or leaning back too far into the chair.
2) Face: Puzzled, little or no expression, minimal eye contact, neutral or questioning expressions. Also avoid the constant head nod, as it can be distracting for the interviewer.
3) Arms: folded, tense or over the chest.
4) Hands: moving in bold gestures, twiddling of thumbs, wringing of hands, clicking fingernails or any other nervous type habit.
5) Legs: Fidgeting, crossed with an ankle on the opposite knee, or facing away from the interviewer.

Your second tool is to practice positive body language.

The key to body language is being, open and positive. You can create a positive and confident message by keeping your body language open. But what does "open" actually mean? Great question.

Think about a time when you were a child. You went to bed after watching a scary movie, and you thought the bad guy or the monster was in the room with you. What did you do? Did you curl up into a little ball or the fetal position? Did you find your arms together or crossed across a pillow? Did you place your back away from the "monster." Why did your body naturally move into this position? Because you were scared and trying to protect yourself, you closed in on yourself.

In the adult world, our "monster" often is our own insecurity, our lack of confidence or an imagined fear of failure. And we also start to use similar types of adult body language. We may cross our arms or legs. We may speak in soft tones. We may avoid eye contact. Each action is interpreted by the interviewer as less than positive. So your goal is to exude positive body language. You need to project an open aura and open mind. Remember not to cross your arms or legs. This is a closed body position and conveys a sense of insecurity or negativity. Instead open yourself up via your body position and facial expression. You can promote a positive, confident presence and message by working on the following key elements:

1) **Your body angle:** Whether you are standing or sitting, just lean forward ever so slightly. By leaning forward, you show you are interested in the other person and are paying attention to him.

2) **Your face:** Don't be afraid to smile. As soon as you come in contact with someone, smile, smile, smile at them. Let them know you are pleased to meet them. Then ensure your face is relaxed. Don't bite your lip, and be wary of eyebrows that are constantly raised. What may appear to be conveying interest or surprise may appear after a while like a Botox chemistry lab gone wrong.

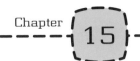

3) **Your eyes:** Make eye contact. Your job isn't to stare someone down. However, if the interviewer asks a question, look directly at him and answer it. You may have heard advice in the past to focus on a spot on the wall directly behind the interviewer to beat eye contact fear. This is your fair warning that this may in fact look like you are staring at a spot on the wall behind the interviewer. If you start to feel uncomfortable from too much eye contact, blink. Just be careful not to give the accidental eye roll when doing so.

3) **Your arms:** Allow your arms to relax at your sides when you are standing. When you are sitting, place them on the rests of the seat. And if you are seated at a table across from the interviewer, place your forearm and hands on the table. Don't be afraid to make large, natural gestures with them when you are talking. Most of all, keep your arms open. Avoid crossing your arms. And please don't sit on your hands.

4) **Your hands:** Keep your hands open. And remember, for both men and women, give everyone a firm handshake. This will project confidence, even if you are feeling a bit nervous.

5) **Your legs:** The recommendation is to never cross your legs when seated. When standing, use a strong platform. Your legs should be shoulder length apart.

6) **Your body:** Squarely face the person you to whom you are talking. Don't look away from him. Stand or sit with straight posture. Imagine a string coming out of the top of your head. Now imagine that string being pulled taut. You won't be asked to cross the room balancing books on top of your head, but this posture will not only help you present better, it will also help you feel more confident. Like animals in the wild, the appearance of being larger (visualize a cat raising it's fur) will convey confidence and give you an air of control.

7) **Your tone:** Your tone conveys your attitude and confidence. Thus, you need to practice your answers to interview questions aloud. Use inflections in your voice and a strong volume. Beware of a rising tone at the end of your sentences. Remember, you are telling the interviewer that you are right for the job, not asking him.

Make sure you understand your new tools, as you will soon be using them in mock interviews.

Chapter Summary

Body Language

Over 50 percent of each message you convey is through nonverbal communication.
Successful job candidates understand the importance of nonverbal communication and use nonverbal cues to their advantage.

You learned about two major tools for nonverbal communication.

1) A positive attitude. You must become your biggest fan. Proactively use mental imagery before each and every interview.

2) Use positive body language and tone. Practice the eight following elements:

- Your body angle
- Your face
- Your eyes
- Your arms
- Your hands
- Your legs
- Your body
- Your tone

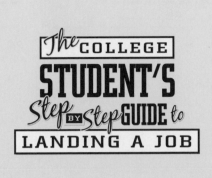

Chapter 16

Crafting A Question

A great question shows your
interest in an employer's
organization and your level of
preparation for the interview.

Great screen writers plot every detail of their film or play in the script. They provide descriptions of the character's personality, their motives and their feelings in each scene. Great screen writers pen each and every detail of the movie's plot, rather than leave it up to the actors to interpret or develop extemporaneously. Why? Because great screen writers know the goal is to successfully develop an act that logically maintains the audience's interest in the movie. And this interest can only be ignited and maintained with a logical plan.

Crafting a question.

As you learned through the previous chapters, an interview resembles theater. You are an actor and a screen writer and your goal is to maintain the interest of your audience, the interviewer. You want them clamoring for more.

By taking this approach, it is only logical that you prepare for each and every action in an interview, including questions. A successful candidate is always prepared with a number of questions that he can access at the right time.

A great screen writer wouldn't film a movie without a script. Why would a job candidate enter an interview without a script of questions?

Why is it important to ask questions?

In a job interview, an employer may ask the candidate if he has any questions. The employer's goal is twofold. First, the interviewer wants to help the candidate learn more about the company and position. Second, the questions assist the interviewer. An insightful question indicates the level of the candidate's preparation and commitment to the position. So let's learn how to display your preparation and interest through the questions you ask an interviewer.

The keys to a great question.

Now that you are aware of the importance of asking questions, the next step is to understand the key elements of a great question.

Preparation: In order to ask insightful questions, you'll need to prepare ahead of time. An interview can be extremely stressful. Even a great candidate faces a challenge to immediately develop an insightful question. Make the best impression you can through fantastic preparation because a poorly phrased or thought out question can be as damaging as no question.

Applicability: The question must pertain to the interviewer and the situation.

Insightful: A great question reflects a researched understanding of an institution.

Genuine: A great question reflects a sense of commitment to the position. You relay to the interviewer that you have invested time in learning more about the institution because you truly want the job.

Where Do I Begin To Learn How To Craft A Question?

First, conduct research. From your research, you should be able to learn key elements about your prospective employer. The more research you conduct, the more questions you will be able to develop. Review the work you conducted as you read the chapter The Difference Between Talent and Genius to gain quick tips on the institution and its industry.

As you fashion questions, remember to add them to the BLUEPRINT FOR SUCCESS: INTERVIEW PREPARATION section in *The College Student's Step-By-Step Guide To Landing A Job:* Career Toolkit. Interviewing and preparing questions tend to be challenging and time consuming. That's why you will find an apprenticeship on the following pages with a number of questions to assist you.

The Million Dollar Question
Warning: This should be your very last question.

Do not lead your question and answer period with this question.

At the end of the interview, you have one final opportunity to make sure the interviewer has an understanding of your skills.

To ensure this understanding always ask "Were there any questions that I may not have covered or you'd like me to clarify?"

This question displays your interest in the interview. Do not worry if the interviewer replies with a "Yes." This shows he is impressed by you and wants to provide you with another chance.

-- APPRENTICESHIP --

To increase the efficiency of your preparation, a gaggle of questions follow. You'll need to review each question to determine the level of pertinence to the interview and the employer. (Please remember, the word institution is used as a placeholder for the company or organization's name). Before you begin an interview, make sure you have a typed list of questions. Bring this list to your interview.

- *Who would I report to in the organization?*

- *Was this position previously filled? If so, may I ask why the position became open?*

- *How do you learn about your major competitors?*

- *I noticed the following _____ were competitors. Who poses the greatest challenge?*

- *Can you please describe your performance review process?*

- *How often do reviews occur?*

- *How does this organization develop people?*

- *What type of people have advanced?*

- *Does a mentor program exist?*

- *I've read the job description. If you had to prioritize the elements of the job description, what would the priority be?*

- *In order to achieve success at this institution, what are the key traits or skills you search for in candidates?*

- *What aspects of the job do most employees enjoy about this position?*

- *In order to understand the institution's culture, may I ask what you enjoy most about the institution?*

- *Could you briefly describe the institution's performance evaluation system?*

- *What's the typical path for advancement?*

- *In my research, I noted the following trends. (Insert trends here). What other major trends do you see impacting this organization?*

- *What do you see as the key challenge for this institution?*

- *Could you briefly describe the institution's reward and recognition system?*

- *Could you please describe the professional development activities? What is the organization's philosophy on developing its staff? What opportunities exist?*

- *Could you please describe the vision of this institution?*

- *What is this organization successful at?*

- *How would you describe the culture of this institution?*

- *I noticed in the news recently, the organization did _____. What was the thought behind the action?*

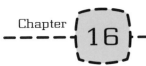

Chapter Summary

Crafting A Question

Successful career artisans are always prepared.
The successful candidate knows the more time he spends before the interview, the more effective he is during the interview.

Take the perspective of a writer of scripts.
Write out your questions. A question helps you understand more about a company or position and displays your interest in the organization.

What makes a great question?
1) **Preparation:** A carefully crafted question reflects the candidate is sufficiently interested in the position and willing to spend time before the interview.

2) **Applicability:** The question directly pertains to the interview and the situation.

3) **Insightful:** The question reflects a thorough understanding of the institution.

4) **Genuine:** The questions show you genuinely want the position.

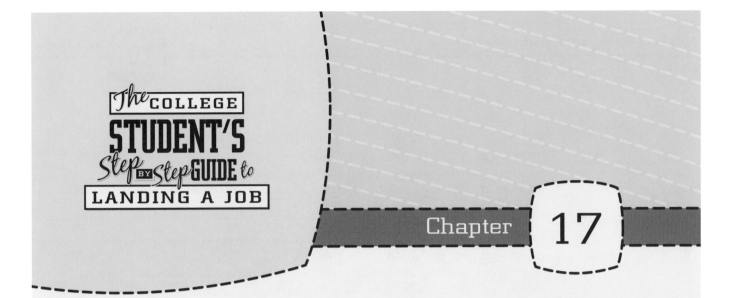

Chapter 17

The Right Gear

You can help create a perception
of professionalism by investing in
the proper clothing.

The proper clothing and gear is critical in essentially every industry, especially in the theater. If an actor were portraying a carpenter, clothing such as a tool belt or carpenter's pants would undoubtedly be used instead of a tuxedo or basketball uniform. The clothing helps the audience create a perception of the actor, a perception that the actor fits the part.

In a job interview, as you can imagine, the proper clothing is also important. As you've read, your goal during a job interview is to create a perception of value. Your clothing can go a long way in facilitating this perception. You want your clothing to show you will fit into the culture of the company. Don't allow your clothing to detract from your hard work and preparation.

Before your first interview, buy the proper clothing to create a perception of quality and value.

Business Casual

Business casual tends to be the rule, rather than the exception in most industries and organizations. Due to this trend, many employers allow or even request that candidates wear business casual attire at the interviews. The recommendation is simple: Be conservative.

Conservative Is Best

You always create a positive impression by dressing conservatively.

Err on the side of professionalism and wear a suit to all of your interviews.

Other Great Gear

Invest in a small padfolio.

In the padfolio, include a notepad, a pen, extra copies of your resumé and a typed list of questions.

Conservative is Best

Your opportunity to make a first impression only occurs once. By dressing in a conservative, professional manner, you minimize the risk of creating an poor perception. Feel free to wear a suit. Suits are always appropriate. Even if everyone else is business casual, you can be assured you will make a positive impression.

Perception is Reality

Make a strong effort to create a positive perception through your dress. If you choose to dress business casual, heed the following warning: Express your individuality after you receive the job. For most positions, being hip, cool, or stylin" is rarely a targeted skill. It would be wise to assume it is not until told otherwise.

Pants: Wear a quality pair of slacks or trousers. Pants should be pressed, unwrinkled, unfrayed and not faded. Avoid Dockers and other cotton-based pants since they may attract lint and tend to wrinkle easily.

Shirts: Men and women alike should stick to the basics and wear a shirt with a collar. Turtlenecks and mock-turtleneck shirts look great on models and celebrities. However, a shirt with a collar reflects on you and your professionalism. Basic, solid colors are best. Avoid sweaters. They create a perception which may be interpreted as too casual. You can wear the sweater after you receive the job.

Shoes: Invest in a nice pair of leather shoes. The shoes should look professional, not rugged. Avoid boat shoes or anything even remotely resembling hiking boots. Loafers or wingtips are both appropriate choices for men. Women should avoid wearing shoes with a great deal of heel - a full day interview might leave you with very big blisters and a limp. Open-toed shoes are completely off limits. Once you've invested in an inspired pair of shoes, be sure to complement it with a new, or at minimum good condition, pair of matching socks. Women choosing to wear pantyhose should bring an extra pair in the event of a noticeable run. Socks or pantyhose are mandatory in all situations.

Make an investment: Invest in a professional suit. You don't need Armani. However, you can invest in a great suit which fits well for around $200 to $300. Again, traditional solid colors are best. For men, if you wear a jacket, make sure to wear a tie.

Keep jewelry to a minimum: In an interview, jewelry for men and women should complement their clothes and not attract undue attention. Avoid ho-hoops and anything that jingles or otherwise makes noise, that could detract from your message.

Avoid tight or revealing clothing: You are creating a perception about yourself during the job interview process. While tight clothing may be all the rage, we suggest erring on the side of being conservative. Make sure the interviewer concentrates on you rather than your body.

Avoid looking like a bag lady: Remember you are there to create a polished, put-together perception. Unnecessary "luggage" such as backpacks, briefcases and purses can detract from that image and project an unkempt or worse yet, a door-to-door salesman type appearance.

DO

Bring a small, professional padfolio. In the padfolio, include a notepad, extra copies of your resumé, your typed list of questions and references.

Allow the employer to focus on you, not jewelry. Consider removing or covering any body piercings before the interview.

Be courageous and don't be afraid of wearing more conservative clothing, even if the employer states the interview is business causal.

Watch the height of the heels on your shoes and the length of your skirt. What is high fashion on "The OC" won't necessarily make a good impression on your prospective employer.

Consider wearing conservative clothing on your first interview. Once you receive the position, you can always consider dressing more casually, based on the corporate culture.

Be prepared. Consider bringing a small packet of Listerine breath strips or a similar product to keep your breath fresh and provide you with a small break. Remove gum or mints from your mouth before your interview begins!

DON'T

Bring a three ring binder, manila envelopes or loose pieces of paper to the interview. Your goal is to display your professionalism and organizational skills to the employer.

Bring a briefcase, backpack or laptop computer bag. Everything you need fits into a padfolio. For women, a small purse containing your essentials is acceptable. Do not dig through the purse at any point during an interview. Items pertinent to the interview should be in your padfolio. Save the rest for the ladies' room.

Wear tight or revealing clothing to an interview. Your goal is to sell yourself, not your body.

Wear linen or other fabrics that may wrinkle easily.

Everything you will need during the interview will fit in a small, sleek padfolio. Invest in a professional classic leather padfolio and avoid anything with logos on it. Keep your red naugahyde free-with-purchase notebooks at home.

Stock your padfolio with interviewing essentials:
1) A notepad
2) A pen, tested prior to the interview to ensure it works
3) Extra copies of your resumé
4) Copies of a typed list of references
5) A typed list of questions
6) Personal business cards with your contact information (optional)

Additionally, the padfolio should have a pocket of some type to accommodate business cards that you will be collecting throughout the day.

Chapter Summary

The Right Gear

Your personal appearance creates an impression in the interviewer's mind.
Pay careful attention to your clothing and the perception you are creating.

Don't fall into the business casual trap.
While an organization may state their dress policy is business casual, err on the conservative side. Invest in a moderately priced suit and pair of shoes.

Remember, no one has ever stated, "Boy, she overdressed for the interview."
Even if the job is for a lifeguard position, a collared shirt, nicely polished shoes and a minimal amount of jewelry helps the interviewer concentrate on you.

Minimize the extras.
Unless the employer asks you to bring specific information to the interview, keep the backpack, briefcase and purse at home. Invest in a professional, thin padfolio. Place a notepad, a nice pen, extra copies of your resumé, a typed list of references and a typed list of questions in your padfolio.

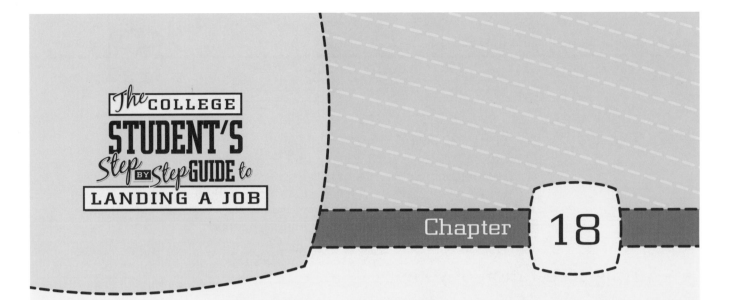
The Dress Rehearsal:
Mock Interviews

A mock interview is the
perfect setting to practice
your interviewing skills.

It's Time to Rehearse

If you ask any Academy Award winning actor, why he or she was able to win an award, you probably will hear him or her discuss the level of preparation involved. Few of us are blessed with the ability to speak persuasively and compellingly on an impromptu basis. And if we truly are actors and our stage is an interview situation, it only makes sense to devote some time to learning our lines.

Strong preparation of your verbal communication skills is key.

However, practice takes time and sometimes we prioritize other activities ahead of our interview preparation. But step back and take a moment. Does this really make sense? After all, you devoted an incredible amount of time and effort learning the craft of job preparation. You learned about yourself, you developed strong narratives using the DART principle and you developed a resumé that reflects you and your character.

Your work has transformed you into a career preparation artist. And your work on paper thus far should resemble a work of art. Why not take the final step and present yourself in an award winning way?

The Mock Interview

The two key challenges to being effective in an interview setting lie in understanding your value and effectively communicating it. Throughout this book, you devoted time to understanding all of the value you possess and you also developed statements to concisely communicate your value.

Now you must gain proficiency in your communication style.

Rehearse!

A mock interview allows you to become more comfortable with:

- An interview situation
- Your style
- Your body language

The Value of a Mock Interview

A mock interview allows you to become more comfortable with the interview setting by answering questions, and interacting with the interviewer. You should plan to schedule a minimum of three (3) mock interviews.

Your Tools: Planning Mock Interviews

Directions: Advance planning is the key to getting the most from mock interviews. The more you learn in a mock interview situation, the more knowledge you will be able to apply in a real interview and the more comfortable you will become with your answers, your interviewing style and your body language.

Timing: The first step in preparing for a mock interview is to work with your career placement/development officials. Request and schedule three mock interviews (each with a different interviewer). Each mock interview should be one to two weeks apart

to give you time to reflect on your previous performance and any feedback received. By the end of the series, you'll become more comfortable with your delivery, the interview situation, and the methods you use to communicate your value.

Depending on your college, university, or technical school, your placement officials will access retired professionals, practicing professionals or their current staff for the interviews. In order to simulate the performance anxiety you will surely feel when approaching your first "live" interviews, it is important that the mock interviewer is professional and unfamiliar to you.

Expectations: Set the ground rules with the placement official during your first meeting.

A) Ensure the mock interview will use behavior-based interviewing techniques.

B) Inform the placement office that the interview must simulate your targeted industry. Provide the placement official with your research on your trade as well as the key skill sets your industry seeks.

C) Provide your placement official with the BLUEPRINT FOR SUCCESS: MOCK INTERVIEW 1 to ensure the placement official and the interviewer understand the key skill sets that will be targeted. You may need to work with your placement official to customize each interview, as you will want to focus on a different set of skills. Your interviewer will use the template to evaluate your performance during the mock interview.

Ask your placement official to replicate the interview situation: Simulate an actual interview. Dress exactly as you would in an actual interview. Bring a copy of your resumé. The interview should last from 45 minutes to one hour.

The Mock Interview Process

The mock interview will have six stages:

1) Greeting. The basic introduction between the interviewer and the candidate.

2) The interviewer provides a brief background of the interview process to the candidate. The candidate will use his/her prepared introduction.

3) Questions. The interviewer will ask a series of questions to determine the candidate's skill set, capabilities and interest in the position.

4) Closing. The interview concludes and the candidate reinforces his/her interest and enthusiasm in the position by asking a series of questions.

5) Evaluation by the candidate and the mock interviewer. When the mock interview is over, the student and interview official evaluate the interview.

6) Identify next steps. Collaborate with the mock interviewer to discuss two or three key areas to improve.

Evaluation: When arranging the mock interview, also request a 15 to 20 minute debriefing session with the mock interviewer.

Evaluation After the Interview: For most college students, their first mock interview is a huge learning opportunity. After all, the mock interview was your first exposure to an interviewing situation. Don't be upset by your performance. Review your BLUEPRINT FOR SUCCESS: MOCK INTERVIEW 1 with your interviewer and give yourself a pat on the back for all of your strengths. Then, select two to three examples to improve. Concentrate and focus on the three key areas, but do not attempt to focus on more than three areas. Progress is best made with strict focus. Your goal is to become better, not perfect.

Mock Interview #1

What will you target during this interview?

Your goal is to become accustomed to the interviewing situation. For your first mock interview, you should try to increase your proficiency in four key areas.

Mock Interview #1

Concentrate on three elements of the interview

- Your introduction
- Your DART narratives
- Your closing

1) **Introduction.** Focus on concisely communicating your introductory story. Remember, your introduction should provide an overview of you. A strong introductory statement should be used to tie all elements of your background in a way that reinforces your value to the employer. Review the chapter on Strong Introductions for additional tips on structuring your introduction.

2) **Focusing on the interviewer's needs.** Read through the BLUEPRINT FOR SUCCESS: MOCK INTERVIEW #1.

3) **Key traits and behaviors.** Focus on concise narratives and believable examples that exhibit your value. Use the DART principle to structure your stories.

4) **Closing statement/Selling yourself.** Review the chapter on closings. Structure your closing to display your past value, your interest in the industry and your interest in the company. Again, be concise and communicate clearly.

Mock Interview #2 (Videotaped)

One of the most valuable methods to gauge your interview skills is through video. Watching the videotaped interview is an honest and in some instances a brutal representation of you. In fact, some students wait a few days or a week before reviewing the tape.

Mock Interview #2

Concentrate on four elements of the interview

- Your introduction
- Your DART narratives
- Your closing
- Your BODY Language
- Verbal cues

However, videotape provides a strong advantage. The video shows you as you truly are. The video interview provides you with a method to evaluate your interviewing skills, your body language, your communication skills, and your value examples.

Planning Mock Interview #2

1) Confirm arrangements with your placement office. Your second mock interview should include a video camera. Make sure to bring your own videotape/cassette to the interview.

2) Ensure the use of behavior-based interview techniques as well as any industry-specific questions. Provide the BLUEPRINT FOR SUCCESS: MOCK INTERVIEW #2 to the placement official at least one week ahead of time.

3) Simulate the real interview situation (i.e. dress appropriately for the interview and act as though the interview were with a real employer).

4) Tape the entire interview.

5) After the interview, discuss the interviewer's thoughts on your performance and identify three key areas to improve.

Key Areas To Target

1) **Introduction.**
Focus on communicating your introductory story in a concise method. Remember, your introduction should provide an overview of you. The key is to tie all elements of your background to focus on or draw out your value.

2) **Key traits and behaviors.**
Again, focus on concise communication and examples that exhibit your value. Use the DART Principle to structure your stories and highlight your experiences.

3) **Closing/Selling yourself.**
This interview serves as another opportunity to hone your closing. Make sure to elicit your interviewer's feedback on your ability to provide a convincing conclusion and reinforce your value as a legitimate candidate.

4) **Body language.**
Body language conveys meaning. In this step, you'll begin to gauge your body language as well as the interviewer's body language. You will also learn a few key tips to exhibit strong, positive body language and other nonverbal keys. The videotaped interview allows you to evaluate and improve your body language.

5) **Verbal cues.**
Occasionally students will use vocalized pauses (uhhm, uhh, etc.) or reinforce the interviewer by always saying yes, or right and nodding their head. Keep these types of cues brief.

After The Interview

1) Wait one to three days before you review the videotape. As you watch the videotape, use the BLUEPRINT FOR SUCCESS template to examine your performance.

2) Don't become discouraged. Remember, mock interviews are part of the learning process. Keep in mind that a portion of your competition are not improving themselves. Your level of preparation already puts you ahead of the competition. Remember the difference between a lead actor and his understudy is generally as simple as the amount of practice and stage time put into the performance.

First, let's examine your body language. When you walk into the interview, your body should convey enthusiasm.
- Stand up straight
- Give a strong handshake
- Walk at a decent pace/clip
- When seated, sit straight, feet planted solidly on the floor.
- Smiling is okay and even encouraged
- The volume of your voice should be level, easy to hear and conducive to the interview space

In the Interview:
- Upright posture, leaning slightly forward to convey interest
- Relaxed, but not slouching
- Be patient and listen for the full question(s). Don't preempt the interviewer. Allow her to finish her questions.
- Be conscious of nodding your head or saying "mmm, hhh" or "yes, you bet or I'd be glad to." This can be negative reaffirmation to an interviewer's questioning.

Gauge the Interviewer
- If the interviewer rephrases the question, she is looking for your answer or you did not express the value she was seeking.

3) Concentrate on three key areas from the BLUEPRINT FOR SUCCESS template and develop a working plan to improve them.

Mock Interview #3

Now, you enter the third and final stage of polishing your craft. Let's take a step back and admire your progress. You completed two mock interviews and targeted six key interviewing areas to improve. Your comfort level with your examples continues to increase and you have gained an understanding of the atmosphere of an interview. In your third mock interview, your goal is to increase your mastery of the total interview. For the most part, you will follow the same process as in your previous two interviews.

Mock Interview #3
Concentrate on the following elements of the interview

• Your introduction
• Your DART narratives
• Your closing
• Your body Language
• Verbal Cues
• Questions

Directions

1) Confirm arrangements with your placement official. If possible, request a different mock interviewer than the individual used in your second mock interview.

2) Use behavior-based interview techniques and any industry-specific questions.

3) Again, simulate the interview atmosphere (i.e. dress appropriately for the interview and act as though the interviewer is an actual employer).

4) Allow the interviewer to use the BLUEPRINT FOR SUCCESS template, mock interview #3 portion in this book.

5) After the interview, discuss your performance with the interviewer. If the interviewer believes you may have some deficiencies, you may choose to schedule another mock interview.

Chapter Summary

The Dress Rehearsal: Mock Interviews

Take the perspective of an award-winning actor.
Invest the time in practicing your interview script.

Mock interviews are essential.
A mock interview provides you with an opportunity to become more comfortable with yourself, the way you answer questions and the way you interact with the interviewer.

Plan a minimum of three (3) mock interviews.
You will focus on a different set of interviewing skills during each mock interview.

Proactively work with your career placement officials in planning your mock interviews.
Discuss your goals and expectations with your school's placement office. Integrate behavioral-based interviewing into each mock interview and use BLUEPRINT FOR SUCCESS: MOCK INTERVIEW templates.

Evaluate your performance after each mock interview.
After each mock interview, discuss your performance with the interviewer. Select two to three areas to adjust for the next interview. Don't attempt to make more than three changes in between mock interviews.

Use a videotape for at least one mock interview.
The exercise is invaluable. You will view your own performance.

Remember, practice makes perfect.
Only the rarest of students will have a perfect performance during a mock interview. View each mock interview as a learning opportunity. Don't expect to be perfect. Expect to learn, to expand your skills and to improve during each session.

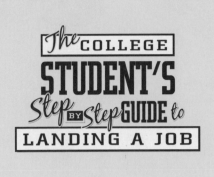

Chapter 19

Successful Scheduling

Landing interviews is fantastic.
Now, you'll learn a few key tips
on scheduling them.

A strategy for scheduling interviews.

An award-winning director of a play or movie invests the same level of attention to all details throughout the entire project, from the initial concept of the script to the number of theaters the movie will open in. The best directors know greatness lies in the details. They understand that even the smallest details, such as the appropriate buttons on a costume add to the perception of their work.

Success lies in the details.
Design your interview schedule with a strong eye for detail.

Scheduling interviews involves the same level of preparation. Is it a small detail compared to the other major tasks in the career preparation process? Absolutely. Could it impact your success? Absolutely.

Many college students fall prey to a major pitfall. They determine their interview schedule with no strategy. In fact, many of your friends may approach their interview schedule in a haphazard way. In their haste, they scheduled their most prized employer–the company they jokingly state, "I would donate a lung in order to receive a job offer from these guys," as their first interview of the season.

> The details of scheduling are simply too important to miss.

Unfortunately, your friends have not yet mastered their craft, their interviewing skills. They were still learning about themselves and their own interview style. Needless to say, they will not provide an award or job-winning performance.

The mistake is extremely easy to make. In our haste and excitement in preparing for the interview season, we totally forget about our skill level. We likely will not be at our best during our first interview.

Therefore, analyze your approach to scheduling interviews. Use the same attention to detail as a director by remembering that every step in the process adds to your success.

Tools for strategically setting an interview schedule:

Step 1: Preliminary research.
Conduct preliminary research about the employers visiting campus. Visit your campus placement office as soon as school begins and request a list of employers. Next, make a list of prospective employers who will NOT visit campus, but in whom you strongly or moderately possess an interest.

Step 2: Prioritize.
On the Blueprint For Success: Interview Scheduling document, combine the two lists and begin ranking the companies. Rank the companies that you covet the most a #1; rank the organizations in which you have a moderate level of interest a #2; and the companies in which you have a small level of interest a #3.

Step 3: Strategically set interviews.
When possible, begin scheduling interviews with your #3 organizations as your first interviews. (We understand many companies' interview schedule may not occur at the right moment to optimize your schedule.) The objective of strategically scheduling interviews is to hone your skill, to minimize your risk and to optimize your preparation for those job openings you really desire. As you gradually build your skills throughout the interview season, you are proactively preparing for the companies you covet the most.

By scheduling interviews with your lower priority employers, you have an opportunity to learn more about an organization which - since it wasn't your top choice - you did not initially delve into with your heart and soul. Often, undergraduates are surprised to learn they have a genuine interest in a company after the interview.

Step 4: Move up the ladder as you gain experience.
Continue to schedule your interviews, progressing to #2 companies and ultimately #1 companies. Depending on your industry, you may interview with as many as 30 or as few as 5 to 10 companies. Hopefully, by the time you reach your most coveted companies, you will have become quite comfortable in the interview setting and will perform well.

Other considerations

When given a choice, also consider the time of day you schedule your interviews. Some people are early birds while others reach their stride midday. While you don't know when the interviewer will be most focused, you can control your self and work around your own personal peak of day.

Generally speaking, the first and last interviews of the day are the most memorable to an interviewer. The same can be inferred when there are multiple days of interviews. The initial or last day would likely be your preference. If a choice is not offered, don't fret. Through following the guidelines in *The College Student's Step-By-Step Guide To Landing A Job,* you will stand out regardless of when in the order you have your opportunity to shine.

A Note On Job Fairs And Consortiums

Job consortiums and job fairs offer a valuable environment to hone your interviewing skills.

Consortiums provide excellent opportunities to polish your skills. Consortiums consist of a number of organizations meeting at a central site to review resumés and conduct interviews. The value of a consortium is often overlooked. Consortiums and job fairs serve as an efficient opportunity to interview with a number of companies in a compacted, controlled amount of time.

Consortiums and fairs offer hidden treasures.
In many instances, you will learn more about an organization you may not have thoroughly researched or understood. Perhaps a job interview with a human resource official may lead to a referral to another department which you may have some level of interest.

Take advantage of job fairs and their benefits.
Job seekers who choose not to attend miss an enormous opportunity to polish their skills. There are few situations in which you will find a building full of prospective employers eager to interview you.

Chapter Summary

Successful Scheduling

Strategically schedule your interviews.
Proactively schedule your interviews. Remember, you want to be at your best when you interview with your most-prized prospective employer.

Conduct preliminary research on employers visiting and not visiting your campus.
Prioritize both types of organizations. Attempt to schedule interviews with your lower-ranked organizations first and interviews with your higher-ranked organizations after you have built your interviewing skills.

Use *The College Student's Step-By-Step Guide To Landing A Job*: Career Toolkit.
It contains a template to help you prioritize and schedule your interviews.

Pay attention to your body clock.
Schedule the interview during your own personal energy peak.

Chapter 20

Other Considerations: Traveling For The Interview And Using Technology

Remember, every opportunity to communicate with a prospective employer is important.

A director for an award winning production coordinates the numerous tasks during the production. Any number of things can go wrong and throw the proverbial monkey wrench into the production's timeline. From an actor's sprained ankle to uncooperative weather that delays filming to living room furniture with coloring that is not bold enough for a set designer's liking, it is a director's lot in life to understand that things do not always go as planned.

Interview situations are not so different. You must be able to plan for the elements that you can control and make the best of the elements you cannot control.

–– Traveling on the Employer's Dime.

For instance you will hopefully have the opportunity to visit an employer at their corporate site. This on-site interview provides you with an excellent opportunity to witness the corporate culture firsthand, but is also somewhat of a foreign concept to the college student. You may not have the experience to know exactly what will occur. So you must simply plan for the elements you can control.

For instance, take the same approach you have had in the entire job seeking process. Treat this opportunity as part of the interview. You should be prepared for whatever circumstance should arise, and there is plenty of opportunity for things to go wrong when traveling.

First, confirm with your company contact how expenses will be handled. Typically the major costs such as airfare and hotel charges will be directly charged to the employer and other incidentals will need to be paid for by you, to be reimbursed at a later time. You can expect that charges for food, travel and lodging will all be assumed by the employer. If paying for any charges yourself, be sure to retain your receipts so that you can be reimbursed. Assuming that an overnight stay will be required, confirm a hotel reservation number with your contact person.

> Always be aware that traveling is most certainly part of the interview. Act responsibly.

Be sure to attain or to prepare your own itinerary. You will want to confirm airline/travel times, as well as transportation arrangements to the hotel. Also note rental car and hotel reservations and their respective addresses and phone numbers. Additionally be sure to have a contact name and number should there be any issues with your flight or reservations that may impact your interview schedule.

It is important to realize that traveling is a part of the interview. Once again, take the perspective of the employer. If you owned the company, how would you direct your employees to be responsible in their business travels?

Be conservative in your travel arrangements. Plan to arrive ahead of time if driving or making your own arrangements.

Prior to your arrival, call the hotel to confirm your reservation and to inquire as to whether or not there will be an iron and hair dryer in your room. If you are making your own hotel reservations, pick a mid-priced room. While there's likely no benefit to staying at Motel 6, getting a jacuzzi suite at the W hotel chain could have repercussions.

If your flight has been cancelled or departure/arrival times changed, immediately inform your contact person.

Once you arrive in town, check into your hotel immediately. The employer may have left a message or needed to change existing plans.

If you will be expected to dine on your own, consider being conservative, but not excessively cheap. If you would not normally eat at McDonald's, you do not need to eat at McDonald's when traveling on a job interview. However, $80 for a 5 course meal is probably excessive.

It is also wise to limit alcoholic beverages that you consume, both for the sake of not turning in a receipt for $30 in booze and to ensure you do not have the brown bottle flu throughout your interview the next day.

Using technology throughout the process

Communicating Using Technology
Just as high definition digital cameras, large screens, and high tech special effects have enhanced the ability to produce award winning movies and communicate a plot in a new and different way, cell phones and pagers have increased our ability to be available around the clock. While technology has made the ability to communicate to others effortless, the same technology can pose problems to candidates attempting to land a job.

Cell Phones and Pagers
The advent of cell phones and pagers has increased the prospective employer's means of reaching candidates. While these tools are by no means required of the student seeking a job, they can certainly make contact more efficient, particularly if recruiting season covers time periods such as summer vacation when you may not be able to be reached at your traditional phone number or address.

There are however, some guidelines that must be followed in order to ensure a professional image.

Tips For Traveling For An Interview

DO

Confirm all arrangements with your contact person.

Keep all receipts for food, traveling and lodging.

Verify your hotel provides an iron and hair dryer. If not, bring your own.

Remember that the organization is making an investment to bring you to their home office. This demonstrates their interest in you as a viable candidate. Take the opportunity to drive home the fact that you are "the" viable candidate.

DON'T

Spend excessively. Consider mid-price lodging and meals.

Forget that you are on a job interview, not spring break. This is no time for a party.

During the interview season, always change your outgoing message. Ensure that background noise is minimal and that your message is professional. You should include your first and last name in the outgoing message as well as additional ways of contacting you if applicable.

During an actual interview, always remember that the person you are with is the most important person in the world at the time. With a clear understanding of this important concept, you realize there are only two options when it comes to your cell phone. The first and most preferable option: don't bring a cell phone to the interview. Leave it in your car or suitcase. How many times have you been sitting in class only to have someone unwittingly leave their cell phone on? The ring is both inexcusable and unprofessional. Eliminate any doubts by not bringing your phone. The second option is to shut off the phone before the interview if you can discreetly hide the fact that you are carrying it at all. Unless you are the President of the United States, you can probably afford to be out of contact for half a day, and chances are the interviewer will not be impressed with your Motorola fashion accessory.

When using your cell phone to communicate with a potential employer, use common sense. Be courteous when leaving voice mail messages for others. If you know you have bad reception, a low battery or a lot of background noise, put off your outgoing call until a more opportune moment arises. Don't engage in cell yell! If you have a live person on the line, simply tell the interviewer or employer contact that you have a poor connection and ask if you may call back in a few minutes.

Faxes

If you are using a fax machine to submit your cover letter and resumé, always remember to include a cover page. The cover page should include your fax number, the number of pages being sent, and a phone number where you can be reached. When at all possible, let the person know that the fax is coming. Remember, an unsolicited fax is not nearly as impactful as a mailed cover letter and resumé. The potential distortion and quality of paper will certainly be less professional. As with all written communication, don't forget to check spelling and grammar. One final note, be sure you get confirmation of the fax going through before assuming it has done so.

E-Mail
- Always use a professional e-mail address.
- While sirdrinksalot@yahoo.com may seem funny at the time, be careful about the perception you are conveying to the potential employer.
- Use your student e-mail account or consider creating a free one from providers such as Yahoo! or Hotmail.
- Always maintain your e-mail; proactively use a spam guard and ensure you always have enough storage space to receive e-mails.
- Check your e-mail frequently. Twice a day is recommended; perhaps at lunch and in the evening.

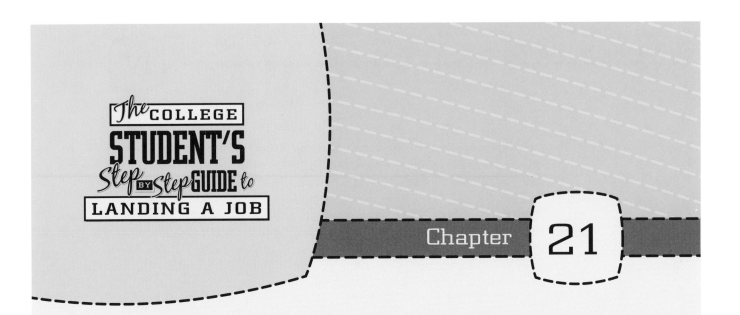

The College Student's Step-By-Step Guide To Landing A Job

For every artist there comes a time when the plans have been sketched, the materials gathered, and the masterpiece assembled. At that point, there is nothing further to do than to fulfill the destiny of the art show and finally the sale.

By completing *The College Student's Step-By-Step Guide To Landing A Job* the book and its career preparation process, you have made a diligent effort to prepare, practice and polish the skills required for the ultimate goal: landing the perfect job. You have demonstrated a willingness to invest your money, time and effort into making this dream much closer to a reality.

Remember that employers seek skills, not just people. By following the principles outlined in this book, you will be able to confidently and effectively communicate that you have the skill sets required. I would encourage you to use what you have learned not only in obtaining this first job, but also throughout your career as you strive to move up the corporate ladder or transition to another entirely different industry. Continue to use *The College Student's Step-By-Step Guide To Landing A Job: Career Toolkit* as you gain experience and add to your already robust skill set.

There is nothing left to do, but to get out there and Land that Job!

Good Luck.

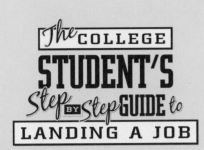

The College Student's Step-By-Step Guide To Landing A Job: Career Toolkit

What were/are your **grades** in:
1) High school
2) Technical school/Vocational institute
3) College (cumulative)
4) College (major)
5) Graduate work

Did your **grades** place you in the top 10%, 25% or 35% of your graduating class?

What were your **composite and subject or subscore results** on your:
1) ACT
2) SAT
3) Graduate exams
   (MCAT, GMAT, LSAT, etc.)

List any **Honor Societies** in which you've been inducted.

List any **academic fairs or competitions** in which you competed. This may include
1) Science Fair
2) County Fair
3) Math Fair
4) History Fair
5) Geography Fair
Did you receive any recognition at any of these events, including monetary awards, ribbons, etc.?

List any **awards** you have received. This
may include awards or recognition for
your:
1) Academic work
2) Creative work
3) Charitable work
4) Volunteer work
5) Student organization work
6) Professional work
7) Internship projects
8) Any other awards

List all of the **school-related** activities.
(This may include your high school,
college or graduate class, student
government, student organizations, teams
within classes, etc.)

List all of the instances you worked with a
team for a class project.

List all of the **charity** activities have you
been a participant. (This may include
national organizations such as the Red
Cross or local organizations such as a
homeless shelter or even raising money for
your local softball association.)

List all of the **civic** organizations in which you have participated. (This may include the Kiwanis, the Optimist, serving as a tutor, reading to grade school children, etc.)

List any other **volunteer** activities in which you have participated. (This may include campus or city cleanup, visits to a nursing home, volunteering at an animal shelter or food bank, etc.)

List all of your **leadership** activities within a civic, charity or volunteer organization in which you have participated (This may include an officer in a student organization, a leader in a volunteer fund drive, a cochair on a committee, etc.)

List any instance in which you worked with a **student, professional, volunteer, civic, or charitable organization** and assisted with major functions including:
1) Decreasing costs
2) Increasing sales
3) Fund raising
4) Increasing profits
5) Leading a committee
6) Leading a task force
7) Leading a group
8) Developing or implementing a new system
9) Increasing efficiency within a group or organization.
10) Increasing membership
12) In charge of the financial area (accounting, etc.)
13) Communicating to the group or a broader group

List any:
1) Musical **instruments** you play
2) Music you have **composed**
3) Lyrics you have **written** (This may include concerts, solo performances, private study or master classes.)

List any recitals, concerts, and locations which you have **performed**.

List any of the following **creative activities** in which you have done or currently participate. This may include:
1) Drawing
2) Graphic arts
3) Painting
4) Sculpture
5) Photography
6) Other endeavors

List your participation with any of the following activities with a **student or public newspaper**. This may include:
1) Writing
2) Editing
3) Layout
4) Publishing
5) Graphic design
6) A creative writing class or seminar
7) Wrote a newspaper article or took a journalism class.
8) Wrote a story, a poem or press release

Please list any instances you:
1) Gave a **presentation**
2) Gave a **speech/attended speech class**
3) Participated in debate or oral interpretation

List any involvement with a **fraternity** or **sorority** (professional or social).

Please list any type of **technology** you can use, and **software programs**. A few examples include:
1) Writing computer programs
2) Using software programs like Word, QuarkXpress, Illustrator, Excel
3) CAD/CAM
4) Engineering applications
5) Desktop publishing
6) HTML
7) Website development
8) E-Commerce
9) Computer languages

List any instances you **developed** a training seminar for others; or you taught a class.

List any instance you **attended** professional training, seminars, regional or national organization meetings.

Please list any participation in a **sports-related** activity.
1) What sports activity did you participate.
2) Did your team attain a record?
3) Did you attain a leadership position on the team?

List any specific instances in which you utilized your **professional skill set**, such as:
1) An internship(s)
2) Working on campus or with a campus organization
3) Working with a business or other institution/company.

List all of your **summer jobs** and your responsibilities.

List all of your **other jobs** and your responsibilities.

List any instances in which you:
1) **Paid for your expenses** to attend school
2) Received a **scholarship or academic award**
3) Held a job **while you attended school**

List any instances in which you:
1) Worked in **sales**
2) Identified **potential clients**
3) Participated in **telemarketing** activities
4) Wrote a **business plan**
5) Wrote a **marketing plan**
6) Conducted a **public relations campaign**
7) Worked to **attract clients**

List any instances in which you made a **recommendation that was adopted**.

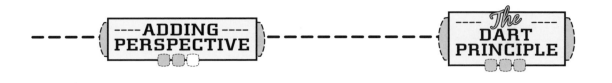

List the results from all of your **personal/performance evaluations** in:
1) Internships
2) Full-time and part-time jobs
3) Academic organizations
4) Any other organizations

List any time you were **named employee of the week or month**.

List any **class** you attended which will assist you in your career.

List any **projects** which you completed/ participated that will assist you in your career.

List all of your **professional experience**, including:
1) Summer jobs
2) Full time and part-time jobs
3) Internships
4) Your own business(es) and endeavors
5) Any consulting you did as part of a class
6) Any assistance you provided an organization as part of a class

List the **reason(s)** why you chose your career.

List any element regarding your field which **excites** you.

List your **career goals** for:
1) One year from now
2) Three years from now
3) Five years from now

List any **past experiences** which you believe will assist you in your career.

List any **major employer/organization** which you think you'd have interest in.

List any element regarding a **specific employer** which excites you.

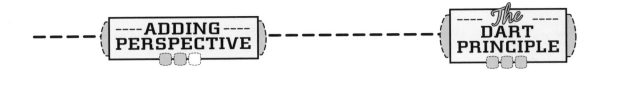

Describe your thought process or method by which you **schedule** your time and prioritize/organize your daily schedule.

Describe your **favorite class** and what elements made the class your favorite.

Describe **what motivates you** in school and describe what motivates you about your chosen career field.

Describe the **method(s)** you use to learn more about your career field.

Describe a time when your **schedule** became overwhelming or too hectic. What did you do?

Describe your **strength(s)**.

Describe your **weakness(es)**.

Leadership
Key: Show facet of leadership

Initiative
Key: Doing something on own: not being requested

Drive, Persistence
Key: Moves forward despite obstacles

Teamwork
Key: Moves team toward goal. Motivates others to contribute.

Communication Skills
Key: Ability to articulate. Presentation or written skills

Handling Challenges
Key: Overcoming adversity

Time Management
Key: Prioritize.

Other Skill Set:

Other Skill Set:

Other Skill Set:

Other Skill Set:

Motivation/Captivation
Key: Enjoy what you do. Gets others to contribute. Challenges both self and others.

Problem Solving
Key: Your approach to tackling challenges.

Conflict Resolution
Key: Listens to others' point of view. Willing to find a mutually winning solution

Innovation
Key: Challenge status quo. Takes risk.

Analysis
Key: Researches the major reasons why something is occurring. Takes broad quantity of information and examines for trends and implications.

Other Skill Set:

Other Skill Set:

Other Skill Set:

Other Skill Set:

Other Skill Set:

Who was involved?
Example: I was a member of a class, a team, an organization, a business, an internship, a summer job?

What was my role?
Example: My title was _____.
Example: My job description was _____.
Example: I was responsible for _____.

When did it occur?
Example: It occurred during/on _____.

Why did I do it?
Example: I was motivated by _____ to do this.
Example: This _____ was part of my job responsibilities.
Example: I took it upon myself to do this task because _____.
Example: This was an activity I did on my own initiative because _____.
Example: Was I one of a few to do this activity? _____
Example: This was important because _____.

What was the goal?
Example: The _____ problem/opportunity existed and needed to be overcome.
Example: I was told to do this. _____

How did it happen?
Example: The background of this activity is _____.
The activity occurred as part of a class, a job, an internship, an extracurricular activity, a team or event.
Example: The event occurred (when?) _____.

What was the result?
Example: The team accomplished (what?) goal.
Example: This was the first time a person or team accomplished (what?).
Example: I/the team received a grade, a commendation, kudos from someone.
Example: I learned (what?) from this experience.
Example: The activity continues to occur.
Example: Someone (who/what?) continues to use our work.
Example: How would I state I made a difference
Example: Did I increase or decrease anything?
Example: I one of a few to receive this honor?
Example: This activity make an impact on anyone or anything?
Example: any quantifiable results occur?
Example: This allow me to enter into or take part in something else?

Key Trends:

1)

2)

3)

Competition and major players in the industry:

1)

2)

3)

Key products in the industry:

1)

2)

3)

Key skill sets needed in the industry:

1)

2)

3)

Key terms:

1)

2)

3)

Notes and questions:

1)

2)

3)

Introductory Statement Section

Closing/Selling Statement Section

Initiative:
1)

2)

Persistence
1)

2)

Creativity
1)

2)

Teamwork
1)

2)

Leadership
1)

2)

Interest in institution

Interest in industry

Why me?

Institution:

Background

Recent News

Company Culture

Size

Competition

Pertinent People

Customers

Trends

Locations

Questions:

Why interviewer chose
the institution

Trends

Culture

Traits needed to be
successful

Philosophy

Rewards/Recognition

Traits needed to be
successful

Philosophy

Rewards/Recognition

If an employer seeks this skill (in bold) you may hear him ore her ask you the following questions. The interviewer may ask these questions. Review each skill set that you have found when you conducted research. Begin writing a potential behavioral-based question for the most sought after skills in your industry by mirroring the questions in the preceding apprenticeship. Then make sure you have an appropriate narrative developed to exhibit each skill set by using the DART Principle.

Leadership Skills

Have you ever lead a group for a school project but were not the formal leader?

The Ability To Initiate

Have you ever initiated a project in school, during an internship or another organization and went beyond the call of duty?

Drive, Persistence And Tenacity

Have you ever overcome another student's resistance to your point of view?

Have you ever initially failed at a project but found a way to finish it?

Tell me about your most difficult class and how you approached it.

Teamwork Skills

How do you ensure contributions by others, such as your fellow students on a class project.

Can you describe a time you lead a team in school or with another organization?

Describe a time when you teamed with other students on a project.

Communication Skills

Have you ever given a well received speech or presentation? What made it so successful?

If you don't understand another person's point of view, describe the steps you take to gain understanding?

Ability To Handle Challenge

How do you handle disagreements with others?

Time Management
How do you meet your daily goals?

How do you ensure progress is made on your school projects or toward your degree?

Ability to motivate or captivate others.
What accomplishment are you most proud of? Why are you most proud of it?

Describe a time you were involved in a university or other organization and needed to move the group toward a goal.

Problem Solving
Describe a time when you may not have had all the information you needed but were required to make a decision. How did you handle the situation?

Resolving Conflicts
Describe a time when you and a fellow student disagreed on a project. How did you handle the situation?

Have you ever changed your style to be more effective?

Tell me how you handle a difficult person.

Have you experienced a difficult challenge during an internship or job situation?

Note to mock interviewer: In this interview, the candidate will concentrate on their introductory statement, their value statements, and their close. Please note, the key traits provided are only examples and should be changed based on the student's needs.

Initial Introduction

Rating:
○1 Possesses low level of skills
○2
○3 Average level of skills
○4
○5 High level of skills

Was the example:
○1 Concise
○2
○3 A strong expression of value
○4
○5 Believable
Interviewer's Comments:

Key Skill 1: Leadership
OR another key skill _____
Rating:
○1 Low level of accomplishment
○2
○3 Average level of accomplishment
○4
○5 High level of accomplishment

Was the example:
○1 Concise
○2
○3 A strong expression of value
○4
○5 Believable
Interviewer's Comments:

Key Skill 2: Persistence
OR another key skill _____
Rating:
○1 Low level of accomplishment
○2
○3 Average level of accomplishment
○4
○5 High level of accomplishment

Was the example:
○1 Concise
○2
○3 A strong expression of value
○4
○5 Believable
Interviewer's Comments:

Key Skill 3: Initiative
OR another key skill _____
Rating:
○1 Low level of accomplishment
○2
○3 Average level of accomplishment
○4
○5 High level of accomplishment

Was the example:
○1 Concise
○2
○3 A strong expression of value
○4
○5 Believable
Interviewer's Comments:

Key Skill 5: Teamwork
OR another key skill _____
Rating:
○1 Possesses low level of accomplishment
○2
○3 Average level of accomplishment
○4
○5 High level of accomplishment

Was the example:
○1 Concise
○2
○3 A strong expression of value
○4
○5 Believable
Interviewer's Comments:

Finish/Close
Rating:
○1 Possesses low level of skills
○2
○3 Average level of skills
○4
○5 High level of skills

Was the example:
○1 Concise
○2
○3 A strong expression of value
○4
○5 Believable
Interviewer's Comments:

Interviewer's Recommendation
Rating:
○1 Does not possess needed skills and history of accomplishments
○2
○3 Possesses needed skills and is average for candidates
○4
○5 Possesses needed skills and is excellent. Above peer group for position
Interviewer's Comments:

Overall Impression/Ability to Perform in the Position
Rating:
○1 Low
○2
○3 Average
○4
○5 High/Outstanding
Interviewer's Comments:

Key Next Steps
For Candidate
Area of Focus:
○Introduction
○Examples of Value
○Finish/Close

Note to mock interviewer: In this interview, the candidate will concentrate on their introductory statement, their value statements, their closing statement, and body language. The key traits are only examples and should be modified according to the student's needs.

Key Skills

	Skill Level (1 - 5)					Quality		
	Low		Average		High	Concise	Expressed Value	Average
Introduction	○1	○2	○3	○4	○5	○1	○2	○3
Leadership	○1	○2	○3	○4	○5	○1	○2	○3
Persistence	○1	○2	○3	○4	○5	○1	○2	○3
Initiative	○1	○2	○3	○4	○5	○1	○2	○3
Communication Skills	○1	○2	○3	○4	○5	○1	○2	○3
Teamwork	○1	○2	○3	○4	○5	○1	○2	○3
Closing	○1	○2	○3	○4	○5	○1	○2	○3

Body Language

Rating (1 - 5)

	Low		*Average*		*High*
Interest	○ 1	○ 2	○ 3	○ 4	○ 5
Vocalized Pauses	○ 1	○ 2	○ 3	○ 4	○ 5
Appeared Reflective When Responding	○ 1	○ 2	○ 3	○ 4	○ 5
Appeared Comfortable	○ 1	○ 2	○ 3	○ 4	○ 5
Speech (pacing, diction, vocalized pauses)	○ 1	○ 2	○ 3	○ 4	○ 5
Exhibited Enthusiasm	○ 1	○ 2	○ 3	○ 4	○ 5

Interview Recommendation

Overall Impression

Key Skills

	Skill Level (1 - 5)					Quality		
	Low		Average		High	Concise	Expressed Value	Average
Introduction	○ 1	○ 2	○ 3	○ 4	○ 5	○ 1	○ 2	○ 3
Leadership	○ 1	○ 2	○ 3	○ 4	○ 5	○ 1	○ 2	○ 3
Persistence	○ 1	○ 2	○ 3	○ 4	○ 5	○ 1	○ 2	○ 3
Initiative	○ 1	○ 2	○ 3	○ 4	○ 5	○ 1	○ 2	○ 3
Communication Skills	○ 1	○ 2	○ 3	○ 4	○ 5	○ 1	○ 2	○ 3
Teamwork	○ 1	○ 2	○ 3	○ 4	○ 5	○ 1	○ 2	○ 3
Closing	○ 1	○ 2	○ 3	○ 4	○ 5	○ 1	○ 2	○ 3

Body Language

	Rating (1 - 5)				
	Low		Average		High
Interest	○ 1	○ 2	○ 3	○ 4	○ 5
Vocalized Pauses	○ 1	○ 2	○ 3	○ 4	○ 5
Appeared Reflective When Responding	○ 1	○ 2	○ 3	○ 4	○ 5
Appeared Comfortable	○ 1	○ 2	○ 3	○ 4	○ 5
Speech (pacing, diction, vocalized pauses)	○ 1	○ 2	○ 3	○ 4	○ 5
Exhibited Enthusiasm	○ 1	○ 2	○ 3	○ 4	○ 5
Candidate's Questions	○ 1	○ 2	○ 3	○ 4	○ 5

Interview Recommendation

Overall Impression

Company Name	Position	Interview Location	Date	Priority